Confronting the German Question

Germans on the East–West Divide

Renata Fritsch-Bournazel

Confronting the German Question
Germans on the East–West Divide

Translated from the German by Caroline Bray
With a Foreword by Roger Morgan

BERG
Oxford / New York / Hamburg
Distributed exclusively in the US and Canada by
St. Martin's Press, New York

First published in 1988 by
Berg Publishers Limited
77 Morrell Avenue, Oxford, OX4 1NQ, UK
175 Fifth Avenue/Room 400, New York, NY 10010, USA
Schenefelder Landstr. 14K, 2000 Hamburg 55, FRG

English translation © Berg Publishers Limited 1988
Originally published as *Das Land in der Mitte.*
Die Deutschen im europäischen Kräftefeld, iudicium
verlag GmbH, München, 1986

British Library Cataloguing in Publication Data

Fritsch-Bournazel, Renata
    Confronting the German question:
    Germans on the east–west divide.
    1. Germany (West)—Foreign relations
    —Germany (East)   2. Germany (East)—
    Foreign relations—Germany (West)
    I. Title   II. Das Land in der Mitte.
    English
    327.430431   DD258.85.G35

    ISBN 0–85496–100–3

Library of Congress Cataloging-in-Publication Data

Fritsch-Bournazel, Renata.
    Confronting the German question.

    Bibliography: p.
    Includes index.
    1. German reunification question (1949–   )
    2. World politics—1945–   .   3. Europe—Politics and
    government—1945–   .   4. Nationalism—Germany—
    History—20th century.   I. Title.
    DD257.25.F7713   1988   943.087   87–26886
    ISBN 0–85496–100–3

Printed in Great Britain by Billings of Worcester

Contents

Figures

List of Abbreviations

CDE	Conference on Disarmament in Europe
CDU	Christlich-Demokratische Union Deutschlands (Christian Democratic Party)
CIRAC	Centre d'Information et de Recherche sur l'Allemagne Contemporaine (Centre for Information and Research on Contemporary Germany, Paris)
CMEA	Council for Mutual Economic Assistance
CSCE	Conference on Security and Cooperation in Europe
CSU	Christlich-Soziale Union (Christian Democratic Party of Bavaria)
CPSU	Communist Party of the Soviet Union
DKP	Deutsche Kommunistische Partei (Communist Party in FRG since 1968)
DM	Deutsche Mark (West German unit of currency since 1948)
EC	European Community
EEC	European Economic Community
ECSC	European Coal and Steel Community
FDP	Freie Demokratische Partei (German Liberal Party)
FRG	Federal Republic of Germany
GDR	German Democratic Republic
INF	Intermediate-range Nuclear Forces (500–5,000 km)
KPD	Kommunistische Partei Deutschlands (Communist Party from 1920 to 1946 in East Germany)
NEP	New Economic Policy
NATO	North Atlantic Treaty Organisation
SALT	Strategic Arms Limitation Talks (applies both to Soviet–American negotiations on the limitation of strategic nuclear arms and to the agreements resulting from these talks)
SDI	Strategic Defense Initiative
SED	Sozialistische Einheitspartei Deutschlands (United Socialist (Communist) Party in GDR)
SPD	Sozialdemokratische Partei Deutschlands (Social Democratic Party, FRG)
TNF	Theatre Nuclear Forces (notion replaced by INF)
WEU	Western European Union
USA	United States of America
USSR	Union of Soviet Socialist Republics

Preface

The 'German Question', which now plays a considerable role in public debate in the Federal Republic, is not well enough understood in Britain, or in other English-speaking countries. One reason for this is that the whole question — the issue of how far the West and East Germans still constitute one nation, and how this German nation (if it still is one) can fit comfortably into a stable Europe in the future — has suddenly become a matter of lively debate inside Germany in the 1980s, after several years of apparent indifference.

Many who thought that the German Question had been settled, perhaps, by the building of the Berlin Wall in 1961 or by the *Ostpolitik* of Chancellor Brandt ten years later, when he accepted Germany's Eastern frontiers and the concept of 'two states in one nation', have been surprised by the flood of argumentative publications and of political controversy ten years further on, as the 1980s have seen renewed questioning of the fate which history has accorded to Germany.

Renata Fritsch-Bournazel has provided not only an eminently balanced and reliable analysis of the historical background to the current German debate — which traces the essential geopolitical aspects of Germany's place in Europe from earlier centuries to the present — but also a guide to the main arguments advanced on all sides in the German debate of today. Dr Fritsch-Bournazel, who is well-known for her expertise in presenting the problems of Germany and Europe to audiences in France and the United States, as well as in Britain, shows how and why the German Question has assumed its current importance in the German political agenda of the 1980s.

As this debate has been conducted essentially between intellectuals or politicians with a more or less articulate point of view on the question, the author has quite rightly woven well-chosen and well-balanced extracts into her text; and these verbatim statements bring the English reader more fully into the debate. However, the book is essentially an assessment by a leading expert of the interlinked questions of Germany's future and Europe's future, which admirably fills a notable gap in the earlier literature on this subject.

Roger Morgan
Centre for International Studies
London School of Economics and Political Science

1

Introduction

The 'German Question' has been a central problem of international relations in Europe since long before the end of the Second World War. Historically, the idea of German national unity was never universally accepted; it always posed problems. Arguments about the precise meaning of 'Germany' did not begin in 1945. For several centuries the response of other European countries to the idea of uniting all Germans in one nation-state had been one of fear of such a concentration of power in the middle of the continent. For these reasons, German unity was not only difficult to achieve but also difficult to preserve.

Throughout all other changes, this central position in the continent of Europe has been a constant factor in German history. For over three hundred years there has been no period when Germany has not to some degree formed an essential part of the European system of states, either through formal alliances or by exerting power more indirectly. The German Question emerged as a wider European issue with the Peace of Westphalia in 1648, which gave an international legal framework to the Holy Roman Empire of the German Nation, a fragmented grouping of territories large and small, under varied sovereignty or foreign influence. A neutralised central Europe, without a focus of political power, remained a first principle for the preservation of peace until the beginning of the nineteenth century. At the Congress of Vienna in 1815, after the collapse of Napoleon's policy of European hegemony, the Great Powers again agreed on a rearrangement of German states in a new, looser grouping, the German Confederation, which they would guarantee.

After the disappointments of the Revolutionary period of 1848/9, the German people in Central Europe at last found the fulfilment of their hopes of national self-determination, not in a 'Greater Germany' based on liberal ideals, on popular sovereignty and the rights of man, but in the Prussian-dominated Reich of 'Little Germany' (without Austria). It is perhaps one of the tragedies of German history that unification was brought about through a Prussian 'revolution from above' and not a liberal 'revolution from below'.

3

However, anyone looking at the historical facts will recognise that the national liberal movement faced opposition not only from reactionary forces within Germany, but from Europe as a whole. Indeed, the solution of 1871 represented a renunciation both of the Romantic nationalist ideal and of the older historical concept of the German Empire. As the period that followed was to show, any attempt to utilise either of these concepts, separately or together, as the model for a more broadly-based political unity, met with opposition from the neighbouring states.

In effect the creation of this densely populated 'Little German' empire introduced a major change in the European balance of power. Bismarck's answer to the Reich's vulnerable position in the middle of Europe was a prodigious network of alliances that seemed contradictory, but was meant to prevent the creation of anti-German coalitions by keeping all other powers perpetually off balance. The system he created for German security was a very complicated one and in its complications lay the seeds of future trouble. Unlike Bismarck, his successors possessed neither the intellect nor the statesmanship to ensure that Germany remained the diplomatic broker of Europe. The failure to renew the Reich's Reinsurance Treaty with Russia marked a major break. It eventually resulted in the Franco-Russian alliance, directed exclusively against Germany, and gave substance to the 'nightmare of coalitions' that had haunted Bismarck.

The success of the Bismarckian alliance system depended not only upon Germany's remaining the balancing partner in so many awkward triangles, but also upon convincing the rest of the world that, in terms of territorial conquest, Germany was a satiated power. In Bismarck's view of German national interest, changes in the *status quo* were possible only if they did not fundamentally alter the balance of the existing system. Those who guided Germany's destiny after 1890 took a different approach. While Bismarck believed he had achieved the most that was possible, his grandchildren thought that the Germans still had to secure their territorial position by further expansion. Wilhelmine Germany was incapable of playing the role of 'honest broker' at the centre of the European state system, once her own dynamism constituted a basic source of danger.

After Bismarck's departure, basic changes of direction in German policy began to reveal once more the vulnerability and precariousness of Germany's position in the middle of Europe. In an attempt to overcome their political problems, the Kaiser and his advisers, in the late 1890s, embarked upon an activist foreign policy (*Weltpolitik*) and an ambitious programme of naval rearmament. The effect of this programme, had it ever been completed, would have been to 'revolutionise' the international system. Not surprisingly, therefore, the other powers, and Britain in particular, responded to this German challenge by forming a counter-bloc, firstly with France and later with Russia, and by engaging the Reich in a naval arms race. The result of this was that, whereas the Germans now saw themselves as surrounded on all sides by envious neighbours, their neighbours perceived them as pursuing a policy of domination. At the same time, frustrated by no longer being the pivot of the balance of power in Europe, as Bismarck had wished, Germany was increasingly a country in search of a colonial empire, unwilling to be left out of the struggle for a 'place in the sun'.

The German 'grab for world power' at the beginning of the twentieth century might be said to be out of phase. The concept of a very large area of economic and political German predominance (Eastern Europe, the Balkans, Belgium and much of Russia, plus overseas colonies and bases) that would make Germany the major power in Europe, and seen in global terms equal to Great Britain and the United States, was historically comparable to the earlier expansionism of Britain and France. But the concept was contrary to the proliferating principle of self-determination and, if successful, would have destroyed the European balance of power. Germany could only have achieved such predominance by stamping out Central and East European nationalism with the help of the military and the police. But in the rest of Europe such repression was no longer regarded as an appropriate measure.

The German government of 1914 disregarded the fact that, for all Germany's economic and military strength, the restrictions of her geographical position should have imposed self-restraint; so a disastrous war was begun, which ended in the defeat of the two Central European monarchies. The European peace settlement agreed on at Versailles, however, in no way amounted to the annihilation of vanquished Germany, as the large majority of Germans perceived it at the time. The German Reich continued to exist, despite tangible territorial losses.

In the years that followed Germany's collapse in 1918, the new republican government was faced with the hard necessity of accepting the financial burden of the Versailles peace terms. To refuse to do so was not within the realm of practical politics; the Allies were not prepared to tolerate non-fulfilment. Responsible German statesmen, therefore, accepted the inevitable, hoping that the way in which they dealt with the Allies might lighten the burdens and modify their treaty obligations. The catastrophe of the lost war and the internal divisions delayed decisions about a new foreign policy. Even the 1922 German–Soviet Treaty of Rapallo was born more from a fear of an agreement between the Western powers and the Soviet Union than it was a definite commitment to a pro-Russian and anti-Western course.

Both Russia and Germany saw the Rapallo policy as an instrument for overcoming their isolation and keeping a check on Poland. To Germany the Treaty had the added advantage of ensuring that the USSR would not rejoin the victorious coalition of the First World War. Similarly, Russia hoped that Rapallo would deter, if not prevent altogether, a reconciliation of Germany and the West. As Rathenau had foreseen, the immediate effect of Rapallo was a stiffening of the British attitude and a revival of France's fears for her security. In fact the German Foreign Minister, a Western sympathiser for reasons that were both personal and economic, would never have associated himself with the Russians had he not suspected that the West was about to make a deal with Moscow that would have been detrimental to Berlin.

Rathenau's successor Stresemann believed that dependence upon the Soviet Union would result in diplomatic isolation and, ultimately, the Communisation of Germany. He was even more determined to preserve her independence from Russia than he was to avoid an exclusive bond with the West. For him, Germany was still *Das Land in der Mitte*; her *raison d'état*, as with Bismarck's Reich, required a long-term policy of reasserting German influence in Europe by steering a course mid-way between East and West. Like most German politicians, Stresemann was an opponent of the Versailles system. Convinced, however, that Germany's revisionist demands had to be modified through an international clearing-house, he sought to achieve a revival of German greatness through the process of 'peaceful change'.

No one attacked Stresemann's peaceful revisionism more sharply than Adolf Hitler. As the leader of the National Socialists explained in his *Zweites Buch* (*Second Book*) of 1928, his aim was not the revision of frontiers but the creation of a German bloc extending towards the East, organised under a personal dictatorship and able to establish and then maintain mastery over Europe. Hitler's quest for Eastern *Lebensraum* differed fundamentally from Prussian expansionism and from the pan-German dreams of the First World War. His plan was linked organically with racism, particularly antisemitism; it replaced the earlier idea of the 'civilising mission' of Germany by the concept of the necessary enslavement of the Slavs.

In the final analysis, Hitler's policy amounted to an attempt to break out of Germany's place in the middle in order to achieve at last a dominant position in Europe and thereby to destroy the traditional system of European states. But in challenging both the Western powers and the Soviet Union simultaneously, he fatally underestimated the limitations of his strategic position, and by unleashing the Second World War he opened the way for super-power domination in the centre of the continent. As a result of Hitler's war of exploitation and extermination Germany not only lost large areas of settlement but, more importantly, she forfeited her centuries-old economic and cultural role in Central and Eastern Europe.

From the start, the major powers who joined in coalition against Hitler were agreed on what they were fighting against and what their goals should be. The first priority was to bring down Germany and to occupy her militarily, at the same time liberating the occupied territories. A second aim was to root out National Socialism and to create conditions that would, as far as possible, prevent German expansionist policies from re-emerging in the future. Discussions of the peacetime aims of the Western democracies and the Soviet Union were more contentious. The wartime Alliance between Great Britain, the United States and the Soviet Union began to fall apart at the moment of military victory, when the factors dividing the Allies again became starkly apparent.

In 1944, the European Advisory Commission, a Three Power body with its headquarters in London, worked out the first proposals for procedure on the capitulation of Germany and for the zones to be occupied by the Allies. The so-called London Protocol of 12 September 1944 also introduced the concept of 'Germany in its frontiers of 31 December 1937', in accordance with the view of the victors that the territorial gains of the Third Reich after 1 January 1938 — including the Austrian *Anschluss* and the annexation of the Sudetenland — had no validity.

Protocol on the Zones of Occupation in Germany and the Administration of Greater Berlin, 12 September 1944 (extract)

1. Germany, within her frontiers as they were on the 31st December, 1937, will, for the purposes of occupation, be divided into three zones, one of which will be allotted to each of the three Powers, and a special Berlin area, which will be under joint occupation by the three Powers.

The second London Agreement of 14 November 1944, which created the Allied Control Council, laid down the organisation of the control machinery for the administration of Germany. During the period immediately after unconditional surrender, Germany was to be governed by the Allied Control Council, consisting of the three (later four) military Commanders-in-Chief, who were to exercise supreme authority jointly 'in matters affecting Germany as a whole'.

Agreement on the Control Machinery in Germany of 14 November 1944 (extract)

Supreme authority in Germany will be exercised, on instructions from their respective Governments, by the Commanders-in-Chief of the armed forces of the United States of America, the United Kingdom, the Union of Soviet Socialist Republics and the French Republic, each in his own zone of occupation, and also jointly, in matters affecting Germany as a whole, in their capacity as members of the supreme organ of control constituted under the present Agreement.

In contrast to these agreements over the occupation zones, plans for the political division of Germany at the end of the war were far from decided. At the conferences of the Big Three in Tehran (28 November–1 December 1943) and at Yalta (4–11 February 1945), Churchill, Roosevelt and Stalin had all called for the 'dismemberment' of Germany; but by the time of Germany's surrender on 7 and 8 May 1945 (in Rheims and Berlin), there was still no binding agreement between the Allies on the division of Germany or the position of her frontiers.

At Yalta, the German problem was assigned to a minor place in the wide range of political issues discussed. The conference ratified the agreement on occupation zones worked out in 1944, which in effect fixed the political division of Germany to the present day, as well as the status of Berlin. The agreement was extended by the creation of a further zone for France. However, no agreement could be reached on the final position of Poland's western border. The Western powers had been unable to persuade Stalin to give up the gains made in 1939 by the treaty with Hitler's Germany concerning the division of Poland. Already at Tehran they had approved, in principle, a westward shift of Polish territory, but at Yalta the fixing of a new German–Polish border was specifically deferred to a future Peace Conference. The two English-speaking powers made their agreement to major additions to Polish territory 'in the north and west' conditional upon the re-establishment of an independent and democratic Poland.

Declaration at Yalta, 11 February 1945 (extract)

II. It is our inflexible purpose to destroy German militarism and Nazism and to ensure that Germany will never again be able to disturb the peace of the world. . . . It is not our purpose to destroy the people of Germany, but only when Nazism and militarism have been extirpated will there be hope for a decent life for Germans, and a place for them in the comity of nations. . . .

VI. [The three Heads of Government] recognize that Poland must receive substantial accessions of territory in the north and west. They feel that the opinion of the new Polish Provisional Government of National Unity should be sought in due course on the extent of these accessions and that the final delimitation of the western frontier of Poland should thereafter await the Peace Conference.

On the day of victory — by Soviet reckoning on 9 May 1945 — Stalin declared publicly that the Soviet Union did not intend to dismember or destroy Germany. Yet, by his decision of 1 March 1945 to place under Polish rule the German territories east of the rivers Oder and Neisse conquered by the Red Army, he had created a *fait accompli* even before the end of the war. In this way he signalled that, contrary to the London Agreements, he no longer considered Germany to be defined by its December 1937 frontiers, but to consist only of territory west of the Oder and the Western Neisse rivers.

With the unconditional surrender of German forces on 7 and 8 May, Allied agreement on the necessary political and military arrangements became urgent. Decisive for the future legal position of Germany was the agreement known as the Berlin Declaration, of 5 June 1945, which transferred supreme administrative authority to the four principal victors. This declaration, incorporating the substance of the London Agreements of September and November 1944, stated specifically that the assumption of government powers and the division into zones for occupation purposes did not 'effect the annexation of Germany'. The joint Allied Military Government under the four Commandants of Greater Berlin was to operate in the same way as the Control Council under the four Allied Commanders-in-Chief.

The already growing conflicts between the former Allies were to cast a cloud over the Potsdam Conference (17 July–2 August 1945), where major arguments arose over the future internal order of Poland and about Stalin's unilateral action regarding the Oder–Neisse line. The Allied statesmen were loath to admit to their own people their inability to reach agreement so soon after the end of the war. In the Potsdam Agreement, which consists of a Communiqué and detailed Protocol of decisions at the Three Power Conference in Berlin (Potsdam), 2 August 1945, all the issues on which no agreement could be reached were resolved by a series of compromise formulae, which were to have serious consequences for the future.

There was no longer any mention of Germany's international frontiers of December 1937, but only of the treatment of Germany as an 'economic unit' during the period of the Occupation. However, the decision to allow each occupying power the right to take reparations chiefly from their own zone made it difficult to maintain the principle of economic unity and at the same time put a question mark over the return of Germany to political unity. Even though the Potsdam Agreement did not finally assign Germany's Eastern territories to Soviet or Polish 'administration', the resolution to defer those issues to a future Peace Settlement was made considerably harder to implement by the decision to deport Germans from Poland, Czechoslovakia and Hungary without the frontiers of Polish territory having been defined.

By the expulsion of German populations, still numbering millions, from the eastern parts of Central Europe, from the former Reich territories east of the Oder and Neisse, from the Sudetenland and Hungary, and by reducing the territory covered by the Reich in 1937 to the area west of the Oder–Neisse line, a situation was created as early as 1945 whereby the highly complex German problem could henceforth be confined to the area of the four Zones of Occupation and Greater Berlin.

The largest migration of people in modern history involved a total of 11.7 million Germans. Out of the 16.5 million Germans who were living in the Eastern territories (including East Prussia) and in

Eastern and South-Eastern Europe at the end of the war, 2.1 million either died or disappeared without trace. Without the Western Powers being able to prevent this mass exodus, let alone stop it once started, the Soviet Union and the new Communist governments of the countries where these Germans had lived tried between 1945 and 1947 to eliminate the problem of minority populations which in the past had formed an obstacle to the development of their own national identity. It was only with the expulsion of the Germans — described in the Potsdam Agreement as the 'orderly transfer of German populations' — that the victory of these countries conquered by the Third Reich became secure. The social burden of this unprecedented shift of population could for the most part be put on the West. However, one must not forget that the tribute paid by Central and Eastern Europe during the outburst of Nazi savagery was particularly heavy. The Jews were the main victims of Hitler's extermination camps, but the Slavs experienced other forms of persecution, such as the liquidation of their elites, deportation and the most brutal forms of economic exploitation.

Communiqué on the Three Power Conference at Berlin (Potsdam Agreement) of 2 August 1945 (extracts)

V. *City of Koenigsberg and the Adjacent Area*

. . .

The Conference has agreed in principle to the proposal of the Soviet Government concerning the ultimate transfer to the Soviet Union of the city of Koenigsberg and the area adjacent to it . . . subject to expert examination of the actual frontier.

The President of the United States and the British Prime Minister have declared that they will support the proposal of the Conference at the forthcoming peace settlement.

. . .

VIII. *Poland*

. . .

The three Heads of Government agree that, pending the final determination of Poland's western frontier, the former German territories east of a line running from the Baltic Sea immediately west of Swinemunde, and thence along the Oder River to the confluence of the western Neisse River and along the western Neisse to the Czechoslovak frontier, including that portion of East Prussia not placed under the administration of the Union of Soviet Socialist Republics in accordance with the understanding reached at this Conference and including the area of the former free city of Danzig, shall be under the administration of the Polish State and for such purposes should not be considered as part of the Soviet Zone of occupation in Germany.

XII. *Orderly Transfer of German Populations*

The conference reached the following agreement on the expulsion of Germans from Poland, Czechoslovakia and Hungary:

The three Governments, having considered the question in all its aspects, recognise that the transfer to Germany of German populations, or elements thereof, remaining in Poland, Czechoslovakia and Hungary, will have to be undertaken. They agree that any transfers that take place should be effected in an orderly and humane manner.

At Potsdam, any question of dividing Germany into separate states was supposed to have been formally disposed of. Yet joint Four Power control, as promulgated on 5 June 1945 in the Berlin Declaration, could not survive the collapse of cooperation between the wartime Allies, as Germany's future became caught up in the struggle for the domination of Europe. As the East–West conflict intensified, so the differences in development between the occupied zones deepened the division of Germany, without any formal decision being taken. At the same time, the Cold War which began in 1946–7 robbed Germany of its historic, central position as a European power. Instead, it found itself on the edge of two frontiers, as the line between the new, antagonistic power blocs coincided with that dividing the two Germanies. Increasingly, the major powers that dominated Europe strove to exploit the potential of that part of Germany within their own control and, whenever possible, to influence the Germany within their opponent's control, as part of their struggle for global supremacy.

The German problem thus became the central issue of the Cold War in Europe. In these circumstances, any attempt to check the political, strategic, ideological and social splitting apart of the German people was doomed to failure. The division was maintained by the determination of the victorious powers not to yield Germany either to their opponents or to German independent control; it received neither legitimacy in international law, nor the assent of the German people.

For the overwhelming majority of Europeans in East and West this freezing of the division of Germany has been first and foremost a source of reassurance, if not of satisfaction — a factor for real security and stability in a world where peace is without legal guarantees. Yet this was certainly true only so long as the division of

Europe was accepted as unalterable. As soon as the East Europeans — and eventually many West Europeans too — began to perceive the division of their continent into hostile military blocs under superpower domination as a serious hindrance to their personal freedom of movement, they had to face the fact that the division of Germany had become the key issue in the political division of Europe.

While so far there appears to be no conceivable possibility of removing these two divisions, historically so closely linked, disquiet about the present pattern in Europe seems to have revived in recent years. This is to some extent attributable to the fact that foreign observers believe the German people — in both German states — to be exhibiting a degree of restiveness that revives traditional worries about the unpredictability of the Germans. Since the end of the 1970s there has in fact been much public reflection on Germany's position and role in Europe. The indications are increasing in the Federal Republic — and in different ways also in East Germany — that many Germans are becoming more conscious again of their peculiar historical, political and psychological place in the centre of Europe.

In the fifth decade of their division, German viewpoints are affected as much by the changing international scene of the 1980s as by the lasting effects of postwar decision-making. At the same time, the Germans' sense of their national and European identity is determined by factors which arise partly from developments specific to Germany, but which are also comparable to similar developments in neighbouring countries in both East and West.

1 / The 'German Question' Reopened?

There are two sides to the 'German Question'. On the one hand it forms part of the intellectual and political struggle between East and West for Europe's future; on the other it is part of Germany's history, and of a depressing everyday reality for the German people, especially in the GDR. For the Germans, the division of their country since the 1945–9 period has meant more than the mere loss of a unified state. More than anything else, it has affected their national identity, that is, the sense of belonging of peoples who, through common history and current interests, know themselves to be more closely bound to each other than to any other people. Thus it is no accident that the Germans' special historic, psychological and political position in the heart of the Continent resurfaced in their consciousness at the moment when détente reduced the confrontation between East and West. This allowed Bonn to free itself from the self-imposed restraints of the 1950s in dealing with Communist Eastern Europe and, above all, with East Germany.

The wider room for manoeuvre brought by détente in the 1970s, coupled with a growing awareness of its limitations, which were felt as painful restrictions by the Germans, led to new interest in questions of their national identity. The close interconnection between the Germans' political and legal status and the wider situation in Europe prompted a great deal of new thinking and writing, chiefly from 1980 onwards, through which the authors tried to prepare the way for the current divisions in Germany and Europe to be overcome, or at least improved.

Yalta and its Consequences

Whenever in history a particularly complex political situation has arisen, one can expect to see all kinds of myths emerging. Characteristically, some of the most powerful myths and nightmares inspired by Europe's history have focused, time and again, on fearful images of what could happen in the centre of Europe. This was as true of Bismarck's nightmare about coalitions as it is for the spectre of Rapallo, the complexities of Yalta or the trauma of Potsdam. While such ideas and images generally have little to do with historical reality, politicians and others tend to judge current situations in the light of the varied historical experiences which they convey.

In West Germany's foreign relations, particularly, the term 'Rapallo' conjures up negative images of policies swinging back and forth between East and West; that of 'Potsdam' the danger of the great powers combining against Germany. Both images had a major influence on important policy decisions in the period following 1945. In contrast, 'Yalta', as the symbol of divided Germany and Europe, has only very recently become the theme of political discussion, especially in the Peace Movement.

A conference was held in Berlin in November 1983 by the Bergedorfer Discussion Group, which concerns itself with political and economic problems affecting the industrialised countries. About twenty well-known politicians, academics and journalists considered the reasons why this historical catch-word had suddenly surfaced again in the Federal Republic. In his introductory paper on the theme 'The Reopening of the German Question', the then Governing Mayor of Berlin, Richard von Weizsäcker, gave the following account of this development:

> On the whole, my impression is that we in the Federal Republic are suffering less from an obsession with the division of Germany than from an obsession with the word 'Yalta', but without everyone who speaks of Yalta really knowing what Yalta means. There are people who say, before nuclear death reunifies us all, we had better unite in the struggle against the superpowers, against those who promote the nuclear arms race. That Yalta created a military no man's land enclosing the occupation zones and has maintained it to the present day. That this situation defines our current political and social circumstances. That the occupation zones turned into spheres of political interest and that this is the basic reason why Europe is piled high with weapons, including the dangerous new technology deployed in this area. That Yalta is therefore the chief cause of today's increased threat of war. And that the German Question in its narrower sense is certainly a part, but not the only source, of all these interrelated issues.[1]

In this view, the term 'Yalta' provides a symbol, rather than a

1. R.v. Weizsäcker, *Die deutsche Frage — neu gestellt*, Hamburg, 1983, p. 14

precise explanation of events; but more important are the lessons of history linked with this concept. The view of a French expert on Germany, Alfred Grosser, expressed in his most recent book, on Germany in the West, is that a new version of postwar German history is emerging, in which the interpretation of the Yalta meeting as dividing up Europe between the two superpowers serves to justify the rejection of the Atlantic Alliance.

> This interpretation leads easily to the confusion or interchange of two very different concepts: on the one hand, criticism of American policy and of efforts to maintain freedom of opinion and of decision-making within a close community of countries with freely elected, democratic systems of government; and, on the other hand, an equally strong rejection of both superpowers expressed as a rejection of any commitment to the values of either of them. This is why many French people believe the Federal Republic in the 1980s is about to give up its membership of the Atlantic Alliance, while at the same time within the West German Left voices can be heard claiming that today's anti-Americanism in the Federal Republic is exactly comparable with France's former rejection of the USA, both in sections of the Left and by General de Gaulle.[2]

It is certainly true that the Yalta debate is conducted in parts of the Western media chiefly by reference to the historically untenable argument that the Crimea Conference in February 1945 led to a definition of spheres of interest and thus directly to the division of our continent. In fact, the *Declaration on Liberated Europe*, formulated jointly by the Big Three, by invoking the rights of self-determination anchored in the Atlantic Charter, laid down explicitly that all people should have the right to choose the form of government under which they wished to live. Through free elections, governments should be drawn up in accordance with the will of the people. For some time, therefore, it has been the contention, of the Americans above all, that what is needed is not the lifting of agreements reached at Yalta, but their realisation.

Declaration on Liberated Europe of 11 February 45 (extract)

This is the principle of the Atlantic Charter — the right of all peoples to choose the form of government under which they will live — the restoration

2. A. Grosser, *L'Allemagne en Occident. La République fédérale 40 ans après*, Paris, 1985, p. 270

of sovereign rights and self-government to those peoples who have been forcibly deprived of them by the aggressor nations.

To foster the conditions in which the liberated peoples may exercise these rights, the three governments will jointly assist the people in any European liberated state or former Axis satellite state in Europe where in their judgement conditions require:

(a) to establish conditions of internal peace;
(b) to carry out emergency measures for the relief of distressed people;
(c) to form interim governmental authorities broadly representative of all democratic elements in the population and pledged to the earliest possible establishment through free elections of governments responsive to the will of the people; and
(d) to facilitate where necessary the holding of such elections.

Public declarations by senior representatives of the Reagan Administration that the United States would not come to terms with the division of Europe brought about by breaches of the Yalta agreements on the Soviet side have given a fresh impulse to the Germans' 'Yalta' obsession, with the approval even of the Bonn government. Speaking at a conference held in the Reichstag building in Berlin on 7 May 1984, the then Bonn Minister for Intra-German Relations, Heinrich Windelen, referred directly to some remarks by the American Secretary of State George Shultz. Mr Shultz had used the occasion of the opening of the Stockholm Conference on Confidence and Security-building Measures and Disarmament in Europe (CDE) to describe the division of Europe as illegal.

> The American Secretary of State, like many European statesmen using other words, put his finger on the heart of the problem. The division of Europe is above all a question of human rights and of people's right to self-determination. The division of Europe is based on the fact that the peoples of Eastern Europe and the Germans in the other half of Germany are deprived of the right of self-determination, the right to make their own decisions now in the present or for their future.[3]

The American political scientist Zbigniew Brzezinski, son of an aristocratic Polish family whose lands now lie in the Soviet Ukraine, is also among those who have recently been reflecting on possible

---

3. H. Windelen, 'Die europäische Verantwortung der Deutschlandpolitik', in *Die Teilung Deutschlands und Europas, Zusammenhänge, Aufgaben, Perspektiven*, Bonn, 1984, p. 11

long-term political developments in Europe. In an essay on 'The future of Yalta', President Carter's former Security Advisor proposed a comprehensive strategy which could help to overcome both the East–West rift in Europe and the division of Germany:

> Yalta is unfinished business. It has a longer past and it may have a more ominous future than is generally recognized. . . . [It] remains of great geopolitical significance because it symbolizes the unfinished struggle for the future of Europe. . . . With divided Germany thus serving as the permanent catalyst for change, the issue of the future of Europe remains a live issue, despite the stalemate of the last 40 years.

Brzezinski's central argument is that, unless the division of Germany is overcome, there can be no true Europe. However, he also makes plain that, while Europeans on the one hand are certainly pushing against the division of their continent, on the other they are not necessarily interested in re-establishing a unified and independent country with major economic, political and, indeed, military capabilities in the middle of Europe. In the view of President Carter's Security Advisor, these contradictions will be resolved only as the wider process of East–West cooperation gradually makes political change possible in the whole of Europe.

> The purpose of healing the East–West rift in Europe is not to dismantle any existing state, but to give every European people the opportunity to participate fully in wider, all-European cooperation. In that context, the division of Germany need not be undone through formal reunification but by the gradual emergence of a much less threatening loose confederation of the existing two states.[4]

This clarification should help, above all, to remove the impression that the West is aiming in the first place to alter the territorial status quo in Eastern Europe. Such fears have been expressed in connection with the Yalta debate, which is seen by the Communist leaderships as directly threatening their own position and power. This applies above all to the Poles who, in view of the westward shift of their country as a consequence of the Second World War, fear any alteration in the status quo between the two Germanies (actual or presumed) as a potential threat to their territorial position. This concern was expressed openly in a semi-official commentary on Brzezinski's plan, originating from the Warsaw political scientist,

4. Z. Brzezinski, 'The Future of Yalta', in *Foreign Affairs*, Winter 1984/5, pp. 279f.

Adam Rotfeld, and commemorating the fortieth anniversary of the
end of the war in Europe.

> What value would assurances about the permanence of her existing
> borders and territorial integrity have for Poland, if a unified German state
> were set up without Soviet guarantees? . . . The time is ripe for the major
> powers to apply themselves once more to the search for common agree-
> ments. It would be sad if the anniversary of an important and fruitful
> effort at cooperation should deepen differences and conflicts.[5]

The Peace Debate and *Deutschlandpolitik*

Even a brief look at the controversy over Yalta makes it clear that
the problems of Germany's future always include an international
security policy dimension also, either for the Germans themselves or
for their neighbours. In the first place, this is because the German
Question is less the cause than the outcome of a number of wider
problems, resulting from the uncertainties of the international situation at a time when neither détente nor Cold War predominates.
East–West relations have worsened appreciably since the end of the
1970s and the system of security based on deterrence has, in the eyes
of many Europeans, become distinctly less secure with the sudden
acceleration of the arms race, chiefly in the area of strategic weapons
in Europe. Such a situation has caused not only growing frustration,
but demands for a radical change of direction, an escape from the
old pattern of alliances and, if possible, from any association with
the global conflict between the superpowers.

The peace theme is a particularly explosive subject in political
debate in Germany because it is tied up with so many unanswered
questions, hopes and fears. In the light of the controversy over
replacing nuclear missiles, the question of Germany's role in Europe
is posed again with growing urgency. There were attempts in the
early postwar years, too, to reject the fact of East–West conflict, to
withdraw from its pressures. This even led to the idea that only the
policy of a 'Third Way' between the two blocs then developing
would offer Germany any prospect of remaining independent and of
preserving national unity. The situation in the immediate postwar
period is not, of course, comparable with that of today's world, yet
for all the differences, certain aspects of those arguments are clearly
still relevant.

5. A. Rotfeld, 'Jalta: Mit, symbol czy zobowiazanie?', in *Polityka*, 26 January 1985

By far the most widespread argument associated with policies for Germany's future is that a war between East and West in Europe would pose particular danger to the German people, irrespective of whether it were waged with conventional or with nuclear weapons. In 1979 the exiled East German intellectual Rudolf Bahro wrote:

> This frontier between the two blocs and the concentration of destructive power on both sides of it — this is what in a crisis would turn our country, before any other in Europe, into a shooting range for the two super-powers. Because this is where the world divides between them, we are the ones in greatest danger, like the Koreans in a similar situation. But for us the house of cards built on 'security through armaments' will collapse first. This is the common danger shared by both German states. They are united precisely on that one point, and have remained so since 1945. So it is no accident that they now seem to be united in one Peace Movement.[6]

A similar argument is put forward by the writer Wolfgang Venohr, publisher of a book with a title both prescriptive and speculative: *Die deutsche Einheit kommt bestimmt* (*German unity must come*). The volume contains contributions by authors as different as the German nationalist historian Hellmuth Diwald and Peter Brandt, a historian with socialist views, based in Berlin and son of the former Chancellor. They can still agree on one point: only when Germany is reunified can the risk of war decrease; German demands for reunification are not only in their own national interests, but in the interests of the whole of mankind. In the words of the editor:

> German unity must come. That much is now clear. Either it will come through military catastrophe, in which case the reunification of all Germans will be in a mass grave. Or it will come through a political solution; German unity will then be revealed as the sole effective guarantee of peace in Europe. . . .
>
> Faced with visions of doom, Germans in both East and West talk of all imaginable prospects but one: the fact that the country in which they all live is the target of both military blocs; GERMANY, site of the Super-Holocaust to come.[7]

When these kinds of argument are used widely, fears that an East–West conflict would pose a particular danger to both halves of Germany are not easy to allay. Yet it is questionable whether the

---

6. R. Bahro, *Wahnsinn mit Methode*, Berlin, 1982, p. 69
7. W. Venohr (ed.), *Die deutsche Einheit kommt bestimmt*, Bergisch-Gladbach, 1982, pp. 6ff.

idea of frontline territories or of degrees of danger differing between countries has any real meaning in a nuclear age. In a situation of mutual deterrence (of Mutual Assured Destruction), the 'community of danger' embraces not only the Germans but their European neighbours and the two superpowers whose troops and nuclear weapons are based in Europe.

The consciousness of a special vulnerability which is manifested particularly in the Peace Movement comes not only from apocalyptic fears of nuclear destruction. A further argument refers directly to the difficult legacy of the German history of this century and from this draws a moral obligation to mobilise humanity to oppose nuclear weapons. At the annual conference of the German Protestant Churches in Hamburg in 1981, which was attended by nearly 120,000 (mainly young) people, this strand of the argument lay at the centre of much of the discussion.

The special duty of the Germans to concern themselves with the banning and removal of nuclear weapons was the subject of a speech made at Hamburg by the former General, Gert Bastian, who at the beginning of 1980 had applied for early retirement from the West German army as a protest against NATO's nuclear arms programme, and in the following year became a leading figure in the Peace Movement, along with Petra Kelly, of the Greens.

> If Europeans, above all the members of small, non-nuclear nations like the Dutch, the Belgians, Scandinavians, Italians and especially we ourselves, took a decisive stand on this, then it could provide the push that would lead to major change. We could turn away from thinking of deterrence with nuclear weapons towards the goal of banning and removal of all nuclear weapons throughout the world.
>
> I believe that no country in the world, certainly not one in Europe, can be more conscious than the Germans are of their special responsibility for peace and for promoting such a step, a responsibility derived from history and from their own past errors and mistakes.[8]

The idea that the Germans have only really to desire change in order to achieve basic changes in their present position, and that these changes would in consequence alter the European scene so radically as to produce the longed-for peace (despite all the political and military obstacles inherent in the current system), this theme lies also at the centre of proposals by the historians Peter Brandt and Herbert Ammon for solving the German problem:

8. G. Bastian, *Atomtod oder europäische Sicherheitsgemeinschaft*, Cologne, 1982, p. 75

In this way the German Question — the question of a German Peace Treaty — becomes the means of bringing peace to Europe. If both German states left their respective military alliances, it would create a zone of real détente and at the same time would make it easier for the two Germanies to work together more closely. . . .

Should all Europeans not be interested in having a peace-loving country in the centre of the continent, providing a link between East and West, whose inhabitants would be freed from the traumas of their Nazi past and of its consequences in the division of Germany? Instead of paying for the separation of West German steel and East German chemicals with the division of Europe and domination by the superpowers?[9]

A third strand of argument in the peace debate which is relevant to the German issue is the much-quoted view of Pastor Albertz, that Germany is in fact still 'an occupied country' in both its parts, and that conflict and armaments are forced upon it by the former Occupying Powers. Albertz voiced this opinion at the church conference in Hamburg in 1981, in a platform discussion with former Chancellor Schmidt; since then he has frequently tried to provide reasons for his contention. And in a letter to *Der Spiegel* magazine, Hellmut Gollwitzer was the originator of this comment on the stationing of Pershing–II missiles on West German soil: 'No German can accept this total subjugation of the interests of our people to alien interests, this giving up of our right to govern our own existence to a foreign government'.[10] These remarks were made with reference to the controversy over missile deployment, which in the West German press led to an awareness of the FRG's lack of sovereignty on issues of international security policy. What is known as the NATO Twin-Track Decision of 12 December 1979 was, in origin, a reaction to the current modernisation and numerical growth of the Soviet intermediate-range nuclear missile capability (SS–20s), regarded by the West as an increasing threat to its security. After intensive consultations within NATO, the Alliance decided to re-store the effectiveness of its defence strategy through modernisation of the American intermediate-range missiles in Europe (Theatre Nuclear Forces, or TNF). Linked with this decision on arms replacement was an offer to the Soviet Union to negotiate the limitation of medium-range nuclear missiles.

9. P. Brandt and H. Ammon, 'Patriotismus von Links', in Venohr, *Die deutsche Einheit*, pp. 158f.
10. Quoted in W.v. Bredow, 'Friedensbewegung und Deutschlandpolitik', in *Aus Politik und Zeitgeschichte*, 46, 1983, p. 43

Final Communiqué of the Special Session of NATO Foreign and Defence Ministers in Brussels, 12 December 1979 (extract)

11.

(A) A modernization decision, including a commitment to deployments, is necessary to meet NATO's deterrence and defence needs, to provide a credible response to unilateral Soviet TNF deployments, and to provide the foundation for the pursuit of serious negotiations on TNF.

(B) Success of arms control in constraining the Soviet build-up can enhance Alliance security, modify the scale of NATO's TNF requirements, and promote stability and detente in Europe in consonance with NATO's basic policy of deterrence, defence and detente as enunciated in the Harmel Report. NATO's TNF requirements will be examined in the light of concrete results reached through negotiations.

While in 1979 it seemed a sensible decision to link military security with readiness to improve political relations, in the aftermath of the crises over Afghanistan and Poland the chances of negotiations taking place became ever more remote. The question then arose, following the collapse of arms control negotiations with the Soviet Union, as to whether the Federal Republic could extricate itself from the commitment on missile deployment, or whether in fact it lacked sufficient sovereignty to refuse the stationing of American medium-range missiles on its territory. Egon Bahr, the SPD defence expert, made his own view clear:

Herr Jodl did not sign away the whole of Germany as an available nuclear missile site with Germany's surrender. The objective right of decision over Germany's existence, through ordering the deployment of nuclear weapons, is not derived from the defeat of the Third Reich. . . .

When we talk about missiles and nuclear weapons, Germans in both East and West try to exert influence from afar, to encourage or admonish, they do not want simply to carry out what others decide. The four nuclear powers' responsibility for Germany is virtually still intact. German rights of self-determination are almost non-existent. Things cannot and will not remain like this. While putting German claims above all others is no good for Europe or for us, to place the nuclear powers' interests above German interests would equally do no good to Europe or ourselves. There is a simple answer to those critics in Moscow and Washington who accuse us of wanting a say on nuclear missiles now, when in the past we kept silent: 'We were not asked, when the race first started'. But when it comes to continuing the race, and modernising the weapons, then they must ask

us. We are becoming more aware of our right to decide for ourselves, at
least in the Federal Republic of Germany.[11]

A Search for Identity

Discussions on West German defence policy, as part of the peace
debate of the last few years, have clearly been influenced by the
difficult question of whether to accept or reject the decision to
replace intermediate-range missiles in Europe. Since the start of
their deployment at the end of 1983, this theme has lost much of its
power to activate people, even if the possibility remains that international security issues could again provide the focus for political
protest movements. A further aspect, and one in the long run more
central to the revival of the German Question in public debate since
the 1970s, is some fresh thinking on German views of themselves in
relation to other nations, their national identity. In fact, the redis-
covery of a national problem stems only in part from preoccupation
with Germany's division and her lack of freedom of action in foreign
policy in a situation of international tension. It is far more a
symptom of a deeper uneasiness, arising both from changes in the
international environment and from the alienating over-complexity
of industrial society.

As early as 1966 the philosopher Karl Jaspers, in his book *Wohin
treibt die Bundesrepublik?* (*Where is the FRG Heading?*) had identified
elements of insecurity affecting German morale which seem very
similar to the situation today:

> Some talk of a vacuum in our political consciousness. The fact is that we
> have no political goals which we feel deeply about. As a country, we still
> have no origins and no ideals, no consciousness of where we have come
> from, or where we are going in the future, and hardly any sense of the
> present except the desire to live as private individuals in comfort and
> security.[12]

A large number of recent books and articles make clear that the
question of a German identity is being raised with growing insistence. What is German today?; Germany's continuing history; the
Angst of the Germans; the German neuroses; the insecure republic; the

11. E. Bahr, *Was wird aus den Deutschen? Fragen und Antworten*, Reinbek, 1982, pp.
    206–8
12. K. Jaspers, *Wohin treibt die Bundesrepublik? Tatsachen, Gefahren, Chancen*, Munich,
    1966, p. 177

identity of the Germans; the search for Germany — all these phrases give snapshot pictures of a mood of mental unease which contrasts strangely with the everyday experience of stability and normality of the ordinary German citizen.

One might conclude from all this that issues of Germany's future provide, to a large extent, a playground for political opportunists and sectarians, and that the renaissance of the German Question is to be found largely between the covers of books. This argument is certainly not to be dismissed lightly, but the relationship between German self-questioning and concern in other countries is a good deal more complex. This is the view of the editors of a study of reactions abroad:

> The explosive potential of this phenomenon lies not so much in the fact that, to foreign observers, the German Question so often appears to be distorted, as in the fact that anxiety about the unpredictability of the Germans is being stirred up with such vigour, after three decades of calm. For this reason, the task cannot simply be to try to correct current prejudices, but rather to detect the many small pockets of fire behind the huge cloud of smoke. Only then can the firefighters be certain of success.[13]

Since the emergence in Europe of the modern nation-state, the creation of national identity has always had something to do with the drawing of boundaries. Thus in the German nationalist movement, from its beginnings in the Napoleonic era, there was a tendency to derive the German identity in the first place negatively, through the rejection of all things foreign. Heinrich Heine was critical of this stance:

> The patriotism of a German means that his heart becomes narrower, more restricted, it contracts like leather in the cold, he hates everything foreign, and he no longer wants to be either a citizen of the world, or a European, or anything other than just a German. . . . There began that shabby, crude, unthinking opposition to an attitude of mind which was the most beautiful and holy thing Germany had produced, against humanity in fact, against the universal brotherhood of man, against that cosmopolitan spirit which our greatest minds, Lessing, Herder, Schiller, Goethe, Jean Paul, which all educated people in Germany have always revered.[14]

13. E. Schulz and P. Danylow, *Bewegung in der deutschen Frage? Die ausländischen Besorgnisse über die Entwicklung in den beiden deutschen Staaten*, Bonn, 1985, 2nd edn, p. 6
14. H. Heine, *Die romantische Schule. Erstes Buch*

A connection was thus drawn between the basis of national identity and separateness from other people, by articulating strict criteria for being different. In the past this had far-reaching effects upon German political culture. However, the Federal Republic made a fresh start after the catastrophe of the Third Reich, seeing its most urgent task as that of reconciliation with the West. Reversing the process described by Heine, people at first did not even want to be Germans any more, but simply Europeans. Behind this lay the extraordinary influence which the USA had upon the West Germans' search for identity. In the disaster of 1945 they lost their faith in themselves and put their trust almost unconditionally in those who had defeated and liberated them, who promised to protect them against the new, Communist danger, and who helped in their economic and political reconstruction. This historical background makes more readily understandable the anxiety of many foreign observers, who suspect that behind the search for a German identity lies a resurgence of anti-Western attitudes. In the words of a Parisian journalist: 'By rediscovering its geography, Germany is reviving the Central European side of its character. This turns its back not only on imports from the USA's cultural 'general stores', but also on its old, close friends, the French.'[15]

However, the problem here may be more apparent than real, since it is precisely because a definition of identity based on nationality is so unattainable that there is now a chance of defining German-ness other than by separateness. Following the failure of Hitler's attempt at world power, and the division of Germany which resulted, the German problem is defined today for West Germany by the two basic facts of Western allegiance and a geopolitical place in the heart of Europe. The basic contradictions between these two facts produce some tension. Through its obligations as part of the Atlantic Alliance, and of the European Community, as well as through its Constitution, the Federal Republic belongs politically and socially to the circle of Western democracies. On the other hand, through being in Central Europe and as a result of division, it has to reach understanding and compromise with neighbours in the East. From the Germans' viewpoint, therefore, they have no sole and exclusive loyalty, but a varied pattern of allegiances. In his introduction to a collection of writings on 'the identity of the Germans', Werner Weidenfeld, a professor of politics at Mainz University, describes this situation as follows:

15. C. de Sarego, 'Géographie: Centre-Europe', in *Libération*, 7 March 1983

In the future, too, the Germans will have to live with an identity which has many layers, corresponding to many different aspects of their communal life. The relativising effect of this may prevent the claims of any one political viewpoint from being elevated to the level of sole way of salvation. Besides social allegiances — those of family, local community, church, and others — there will be the consciousness of belonging to a country, be it the Federal Republic of Germany or the German Democratic Republic. And there will also be the desire for a political community of all Germans, the pressure for self-determination for all Germans. . . . On top of that, the European perspective will add a further layer to the German identity: from a recognition that many problems go beyond national boundaries and can only be overcome internationally; and from a realisation that peace can only be secured through common effort and that the needs and challenges of our time demand international solidarity.[16]

The Problem of Conflicting Goals

When the Federal Republic of Germany and the German Democratic Republic were founded in 1949 the German people could still hope that the Soviet Union would one day withdraw from Central Europe and leave the way clear for a peace treaty. Since then the basic facts of the situation have altered considerably. Four decades after the end of the Second World War there is no prospect in sight of overcoming the divisions of Europe and Germany, even though there are as good grounds now as there were then for refusing to accept the existing situation.

In the 1950s international relations for West Germany meant, in practical terms, relations with the West. The series of agreements signed with the East European countries in the early 1970s, while certainly not loosening the older and more important ties with the West, did lay the groundwork for a new pattern of links with the East. For both Adenauer and Brandt, the Federal Republic had to adapt to external constraints, in the former case in order to free itself from a situation of powerlessness and, for the latter, in order to combat the diplomatic isolation which arose in the 1960s as a result of the relaxation of tension between East and West.

In the period of détente, nearly all the countries of Europe, including the two German states, gained room for manoeuvre which they had not had previously. By contrast, in the ensuing period of

16. W. Weidenfeld (ed.), *Die Identität der Deutschen*, Munich, 1983, pp. 42–3

renewed confrontation between the United States and the Soviet Union, European chances of achieving their own foreign policy goals have been reduced. This is especially painful for West Germany, which has an even stronger interest than its NATO partners in maintaining continuity in relations with the East. Whereas for other Western countries, *Ostpolitik* forms merely a part (though an important one) of a wider range of foreign policy options, it represents considerably more for the Federal Republic, since relations with the East are bound up with such central issues of national policy as concern over West Berlin and solidarity with the East Germans. Moreover, détente policies have an additional, concrete content for West Germany, with regard to improving human rights and freedom of movement and the further development of economic relations with Eastern Europe.

In recent times, many observers of German affairs have seemed sceptical about the practical possibilities of balancing out all the different components of West Germany's foreign policy, an exercise akin to keeping a lot of balls in the air at the same time. In an essay on the 'shifting foundation' of the Alliance, the French political scientist Pierre Hassner has written:

> In a sense the West German desire to eat one's cake and have it too is only an expression of the unique situation of West Germany, which makes it impossible for Bonn to commit itself completely to any of the three possible futures: Atlantic, West European, or central European. But in its attempt to combine all three, it needs to be reminded of two things. Some circumstances do impose definite priorities. West Germany cannot ignore the urgent challenges created by the growing external power and internal crisis of the Soviet empire and by the current evolution of American society. They must take precedence over the German dialogue, even though the latter can never be sacrificed. And to the extent that the West Germans engage alone in a dialogue with an East Germany controlled by the USSR, they risk allowing Moscow to manipulate them into becoming the prisoners and the instruments of this triangular relationship.[17]

Other authors frequently express the view that history has long ago rendered irreconcilable the twin goals put forward in the West German Constitution, which exhorts the German people to 'achieve the unity and freedom of Germany' and 'to serve world peace as an equal partner in a united Europe'. The Berlin political scientist Helmut Wagner asks:

17. P. Hassner, 'The Shifting Foundation', in *Foreign Policy*, Fall 1982, p. 19

Does the achievement of Western European unity not mean the perpetual division of Germany? And the realisation of German unity the perpetuation of European disunity? Logically, a United Europe which was not confined to Western Europe would end Germany's division. And surely German reunification, (unless it was made conditional on non-integration in Europe), would not necessarily stand in the way of a United Europe. But is either proposition realistic?[18]

In a lecture given to the Protestant Academy at Arnoldshain, Günter Gaus, first Head of the Federal Republic's Permanent Mission in East Berlin, gave the following reply to such questions:

The European Community is certainly needed economically, but the way it is run, it could not help in the least to solve our basic problem. Taking the long view, it often seems even to be working against it. . . . The time has come when every measure which has to be decided on in Brussels should be routinely and exhaustively checked on in Bonn to see what significance it might have for divided Germany. Decisions taken day by day which affect Germany's future should be governed by German priorities.[19]

As these samples from the recent debate make clear, the expression the 'German Question' covers a range of widely differing issues and expectations. It is less than ever confined to Germany, nor exclusively a problem of the present day. Only by setting more recent events in the context of historical continuity is it possible to give a cautious answer on whether in the 1980s the German Question really is in the process of being reopened.

---

18. H. Wagner, 'Europagesinnung und Europapolitik', in E. Jesse (ed.), *Bundesrepublik Deutschland und Deutsche Demokratische Republik. Die beiden deutschen Staaten im Vergleich*, Bonn, 1980, pp. 149f.
19. G. Gaus, *Texte zur deutschen Frage*, Darmstadt/Neuwied, 1981, pp. 43f.

2 / Europe between Détente and Crisis

'Détente', as defined by the French encyclopaedic dictionary *Le Petit Robert*, is the opposite of 'tension', meaning both 'the easing of strain' and the 'agreeable state resulting from this'. As a word much used in present-day politics, it stands for a 'reduction of international tensions' and is equated with 'policies of coexistence and relaxation of tension'. Such definitions show clearly the many-sided nature of the concept of 'détente', covering both objective changes in the quality of international relations and the subjective experience of the actors involved in various ways in détente policies.

There were periods of reduced international tension even in the 1950s and the term 'détente' surfaced in the media as early as 1955, in the context of the Geneva Summit Conference, but it was only in the 1960s that a real loosening-up of relations between East and West occurred. The two crises over Cuba and Berlin made it plain that the basic ground rules of global East–West conflict had changed fundamentally. In an age when both superpowers had developed comprehensive strategic nuclear capabilities, it became increasingly clear that no longer could a major war be waged with all available military means, as an instrument of policy. It therefore became necessary to find non-military methods of conflict resolution, and to alleviate the continuing clash of opposing interests through some degree of cooperation.

Since détente does not signify the removal of what in fact are continuing sources of tension in East–West relations, even the 'agreeable state' which, according to the *Petit Robert*, should result from détente, is limited by the perceptions of threat felt subjectively by the political actors. A basic readiness to pursue policies which make for a *modus vivendi* suited to the conditions of the nuclear age, can be seen in the search for a *modus non moriendi*. This has certainly narrowed the scope and content of East–West conflict which is based on a contest for political power and ideological supremacy. Nevertheless, there is still room left for rivalry and friction between the two power blocs.

There is invariably a risk to détente when shifts in the global balance of power seriously alter the ratio of costs and benefits for one or more states involved in the process, so that the disadvantages appear to outweigh the advantages accruing from détente. The balance can be disturbed in this way either through practical changes of a military, political or economic kind which put the existing power relationships in question, or from disappointments arising as a result of exaggerated expectations of the concrete outcomes of certain détente strategies. The quarrels between Western Europe and the United States over détente policies towards the Eastern bloc are directly connected with differing assessments of the situation which had developed in the 1970s.

The Parameters of Détente in Europe

Two world powers such as the Soviet Union and the USA, whose international and domestic goals conflict, are nevertheless prepared to cooperate so long as two main conditions are fulfilled. They must, at least in some limited areas of interest, be pursuing identical or similar goals, and they must be able to start from negotiating positions of equal strength. Both conditions appeared to obtain at the beginning of the 1970s.

The first phase of the new policy approach brought a large number of agreements between the USA and USSR and made possible the process of normalisation then also beginning between East and West in Europe. A good many of the agreements reached in the years 1970–3 covered economic cooperation and exchanges in the scientific and technical as well as cultural fields. However, the most important agreements were those concerning the political and military relationship between the two superpowers. The highpoint of détente was the Moscow Summit Conference of May 1972. This saw the signature of the first agreement on the limitation of strategic weapons (SALT I) and a declaration as to the basic principles of détente in which both sides gave assurances of respect for the equality of their rights and on the exercise of restraint. One year later came the agreement on the prevention of nuclear war in which the USA and USSR committed themselves to immediate consultations if the global situation offered the risk of nuclear conflict between the superpowers.

Henry Kissinger, President Nixon's Security Advisor, who had a decisive influence on the American concept of détente, writes this in his memoirs about the May 1972 summit:

> The fundamental achievement was to sketch the outline on which coexist-
> ence between the democracies and the Soviet system must be based.
> SALT embodied our conviction that a wildly spiraling nuclear arms race
> was in no country's interest and enhanced no one's security; the 'Basic
> Principles' gave at least verbal expression to the necessity of responsible
> political conduct. . . . We were involved in a delicate balancing act: to be
> committed to peace without letting the quest for it become a form of
> moral disarmament, surrendering all other values; to be prepared to
> defend freedom while making clear that unconstrained rivalry could risk
> everything, including freedom, in a nuclear holocaust.[1]

The high point of the détente period in 1972–3 was soon followed by
disillusionment. In the next few years, both superpowers saw
détente as increasingly threatened by the policies which their opponent followed in practice. The Soviet Union, for its part, was
committing itself ever more strongly outside its established areas of
influence. Its sphere of activity had expanded because in the inter-
val, as a result of deliberate arms policies, it had reached a level of
military potential equal to that of the USA. From the mid-1970s
onwards the Americans, for their part, saw the real value of détente
increasingly in terms of establishing human rights in communist
countries and accordingly made demands which were hard for the
Soviet Union to fulfil. Finally, Soviet behaviour caused American
business leaders to lose interest in developing trade relations, as
expectations of the results linked with détente by the Soviet Union
were repeatedly disappointed.

Not only American–Soviet relations were affected by the transition from confrontation to an era of negotiation such as occurred at
the beginning of the 1970s; the relationship between the USA and its
NATO partners in Europe was also affected. As the East–West
conflict of the 1960s diminished, questions arose about the future of the
Atlantic Alliance, created as it had been at the height of the Cold War.

If the Alliance was to fulfil its military purpose, and not be
rendered superfluous by the advancing *rapprochement* between East
and West, then its role had to be redefined so that it would not be
impeded by détente. The Alliance could, moreover, be made to serve
as a framework within which the national détente strategies of the
various partners might be linked together and — as far as possible
— transformed into a common NATO policy.

1. H. Kissinger, *The White House Years*, London, 1979, pp. 1, 253–4

The basic guidelines for managing NATO's relations with the East had been set out in the Harmel Report, issued by the NATO foreign ministers on 14 December 1967. The report describes détente not as the final goal, but as part of a long-term process of improving relations and furthering the settlement of outstanding European issues, central among which was the question of Germany. From this emerged the twin bulwarks of NATO philosophy — deterrence and defence on the one hand, negotiation and détente on the other — which would form the basis of future common policies. Lothar Ruehl, currently Permanent Secretary in the Bonn Defence Ministry, at that time saw the reasons for this NATO initiative as follows:

> A number of governments had reached the conclusion, with the passage of time after the end of the crisis period of 1962–3, that besides the negative task of 'deterrence' of an attack on NATO territory — especially Western Europe — and the collective defence function inseparable from that, their alliance ought also to take on a more positive role, directed towards peace. In Western Europe generally, interest grew in easing the situation of conflict in relations with the Soviet Union and Eastern Europe which had survived from the Cold War period. The idea also gained ground that European security in its widest sense would have to be organised in collaboration with the 'potential enemies' in the East. To achieve either objective, the need was seen for NATO to present itself in a more positive light, not only towards the outside world, but also towards its own domestic populations.[2]

The Harmel Report took up a number of ideas previously evolved in individual Western states: the idea first thrown out by President Johnson, of 'bridge-building' between East and West; President de Gaulle's concept of 'détente–entente–cooperation'; and the principle developed by the then West German Foreign Minister, Willy Brandt, of a 'peaceful order in Europe'. This was also the context for the Federal Republic's change of course in its relations with Eastern Europe and East Germany, decided on by the coalition of Social Democrats and Liberals in government from 1969.

---

2. L. Ruehl, 'Die neuen Ziele im Atlantischen Bündnis und die Fortsetzung der westlichen Détentepolitik nach Prag', in *Die Internationale Politik 1968–1969*, *Jahrbücher des Forschungsinstituts der Deutschen Gesellschaft für Auswärtige Politik*, Munich/Vienna, 1974, p. 341

Report on the Future Tasks of the Alliance (Harmel Report) 14 December 1967 (extract)

The Atlantic Alliance has two main functions. Its first function is to maintain adequate military strength and political solidarity to deter aggression and other forms of pressure and to defend the territory of member countries if aggression should occur. Since its inception, the Alliance has successfully fulfilled this task. But the possibility of a crisis cannot be excluded as long as the central political issues in Europe, first and foremost the German Question, remain unsolved. Moreover, the situation of instability and uncertainty still precludes a balanced reduction of military forces. Under these conditions, the Allies will maintain as necessary, a suitable military capability to assure the balance of forces, thereby creating a climate of stability, security and confidence.

In this climate the Alliance can carry out its second function, to pursue the search for progress towards a more stable relationship in which the underlying political issues can be solved. Military security and a policy of détente are not contradictory but complementary. . . .

No peaceful order in Europe is possible without a major effort by all concerned. The evolution of Soviet and East European policies gives ground for hope that those governments may eventually come to recognize the advantages to them of collaborating in working towards a peaceful settlement. But no final and stable settlement in Europe is possible without a solution of the German question which lies at the heart of present tensions in Europe. Any such settlement must end the unnatural barriers between Eastern and Western Europe, which are most clearly and cruelly manifested in the division of Germany.

The German Contribution to Conflict Resolution in Europe

NATO's newly-adopted twin goals of defence and détente had more far-reaching consequences for the Federal Republic than for any other member of the Alliance. In Europe at least, this country was the first and most directly affected, as regards its former policy objectives, by the changed international ground rules and way of thinking. Until the 1960s the Federal Republic had tried to harness every issue to the achievement of its primary goal of reunification and self-determination, thus binding East–West relations to a solution of the German question. But Bonn's function as a doorkeeper on East–West issues became obsolete when other Western powers, above all the USA, gave a low priority to German unity while accepting, at least provisionàlly, the status quo in Europe.

The objectives of the government headed by Brandt and Scheel in its 'new *Ostpolitik*' are described by Berndt von Staden, from 1970 to 1973 head of the Political Department in the West German foreign office:

> Being a regional power of medium size and part of a divided nation straddling the divide between East and West in Europe, Germany had to put its relations with its East European neighbours and with the Soviet Union on a normal footing, to ensure the security and viability of Berlin, to make division more bearable by cooperating with the GDR on a wide variety of levels, to preserve the sense of belonging together of the people of both German states, and to carry all this through without giving up the claim of the German people to free self-determination.[3]

Matters to be dealt with in West Germany's relations with the Soviet Union were the inviolable nature of existing frontiers in Europe and Berlin's viability and access routes. As for Poland, the Oder–Neisse line was to be respected as the Western frontier. The key points in relations with East Germany were the recognition of the existence of the other German state, and various practical issues arising from the survival of links between families and individuals in the two halves of Germany. Finally, in the case of Czechoslovakia, there were problems concerning the validity of the Munich Agreement of September 1938, and humanitarian questions.

Excerpts from the Federal Republic's Agreements with East European Countries (*Ostverträge*)

Treaty between the Federal Republic of Germany and the Union of Soviet Socialist Republics (Moscow Treaty), 12 August 1970

The Moscow Treaty strives for normalisation and détente in Europe on the basis of the 'actual situation existing in this region' (Art. 1). In accordance with the Charter of the United Nations, the Federal Republic and the USSR undertake to refrain from the threat or use of force (Art. 2). From this ban on the use of force is derived the regulation on frontiers and on territorial integrity, which commits the Federal Republic to respect 'the frontiers of all States in Europe

---

3. B.v. Staden, 'Das Management der Ost–West–Beziehungen', in K. Kaiser and H.-P. Schwarz (eds.), *Weltpolitik. Strukturen–Akteure–Perspektiven*, Bonn, 1985, p. 121

as inviolable . . . including the Oder–Neisse line which forms the western frontier of the People's Republic of Poland and the frontier between the Federal Republic of Germany and the German Democratic Republic'.

The Western powers in an exchange of Notes regarded their 'rights and responsibilities in relation to Berlin and to Germany as a whole [as] not affected'.

Treaty between the Federal Republic of Germany and the People's Republic of Poland on the basis of the normalisation of their mutual relations (Warsaw Treaty), 7 December 1970

In the Warsaw Treaty the Federal Republic and the People's Republic of Poland state 'in mutual agreement that the existing boundary line . . . shall constitute the western State frontier of the People's Republic of Poland'. Both partners 'reaffirm the inviolability of their existing frontiers now and in the future' and declare 'that they have no territorial claims whatsoever against each other and that they will not assert such claims in the future' (Art. 1).

In a Note to the three Western powers, the Federal Republic refers to the fact that 'it can only negotiate in the name of the Federal Republic' and that the Treaty does not affect the 'rights and responsibilities' of the Four Powers. For their part the three Western powers declare in an exchange of Notes that the Treaty 'does not affect and cannot affect' the rights and responsibilities of the Four Powers.

Quadripartite Agreement on Berlin, 3 September 1971

The Federal Republic was not directly involved in the agreement of the Four Powers on Berlin. From the beginning, however, a satisfactory Berlin settlement was a precondition for the treaties with the East. Bonn's efforts to pursue its Eastern policy were anchored firmly in the attempts by the West and the Soviet Union, acting on the basis of their rights and responsibilities, and of their wartime and postwar decisions, to achieve practical improvements in the existing situation in the divided former capital of Germany.

The most important requirement for the legal relationship between West Berlin and the Federal Republic is contained in Pt II(B) of the Agreement: the three Western powers declare 'that the ties between the western sectors of Berlin and the Federal Republic of Germany will be maintained and developed, taking into account that these sectors continue not to be a constituent part of the Federal Republic of Germany and not to be governed by it'.

Within the framework of the Quadripartite Agreement the signatories also endorsed agreements and regulations drawn up by the responsible authorities in both German states, in particular relating to travel to and from Berlin and the possibility of visits by West Berliners to East Berlin and the GDR.

Treaty on the Bases of Relations between the German Democratic Republic and the Federal Republic of Germany (Basic Treaty), 21 December 1972

The Basic Treaty, 'notwithstanding the different views' of both sides 'on fundamental matters, including the national question' (Preamble), creates conditions for the development of mutual cooperation on a wide range of levels. The two German states agreed to develop 'normal good-neighbourly relations with each other on the basis of equal rights' (Art. 1). They 'affirm the inviolability now and in the future of the frontier existing between them, and undertake fully to respect each other's territorial integrity' (Art. 3); they 'proceed from the consideration that neither of the two states may represent the other in international affairs or act on its behalf' (Art. 4) and that 'the sovereign power of either state shall be confined to its respective territory' (Art. 6).

Treaty on Mutual Relations between the Federal Republic of Germany and the Czechoslovakian Socialist Republic (Prague Treaty), 11 December 1973

The Prague Treaty was concerned chiefly with a matter on which the Federal Republic and Czechoslovakia took differing views, that is, how to take account of the *de facto* ending of the Munich Agreement of 29 September 1938. Whereas the CSSR wanted a declaration that the agreement was invalid *ex tunc*, that is, from the beginning, the Federal Republic could not accede to this, given the unacceptable consequences which would result for the Sudetenland Germans.

In the end the two sides agreed to declare 'under the present Treaty' the Munich Agreement to be 'void with regard to their mutual relations' (Art. 1), while the Treaty would 'not affect the legal effects on natural or legal persons of the law as applied in the period between 30 September 1938 and 9 May 1945' (Art. 2). The question was left open as to how the territorial sovereignty of the Czechoslovak state was derived in international law.

In each agreement, all the essentials of Germany's legal position regarding its frontiers of 31 December 1937 are safeguarded through a clause specifying that it 'shall not affect' international arrangements concluded previously (Art. 4, Moscow and Warsaw Treaties; Art. 9 of the Basic Treaty; para. 3, Pt I, of the Quadripartite Agreement on Berlin), since agreement on a peace treaty is still outstanding and until then the rights and responsibilities of the Four Powers with regard to Berlin and the whole of Germany continue. In the *Letters on German Unity* on conclusion of the Moscow Treaty and the Basic Treaty, the Federal Republic stated that the treaties did not contradict the political goal of the Federal Republic 'to work for a situation of peace in Europe, in which the German people will regain their unity with freedom of self-determination'.

By their two-fold character, covering the renunciation of force and agreement on cooperation, the series of agreements reached with the East between 1970 and 1973 were a major contribution to the reduction of European tensions. Questions of international security in Europe could now be brought into the open and discussed, free from the burden of unrecognised or politically disputed frontiers in Central Europe and from the assumption that the Federal Republic and its allies wished to contest the GDR's right of existence. Following the Eastern agreements the Soviet Union could no longer, as formerly, represent the problem of European security exclusively as a problem of security against Germany, against a German threat to peace in Europe. A quarter of a century after the founding of the Federal Republic, the Berlin political scientist Richard Löwenthal could comment:

> The opposition between the political systems in East and West provided the basis of a conflict with the Soviets which was *shared* by the Western powers and the West Germans, in which priority was given to pursuit of internal development in freedom and security on this side of the divide. But demands for reunification by free Germans in the West, and for the review of the Eastern frontiers, were the basis of a *particular* quarrel which the FRG had with the Soviet Union and the Soviet bloc, in which Bonn could count on Western support only on certain conditions and, as time went on, to a decreasing extent. The history of the gradual change in West Germany's policy towards the East over a quarter of a century is the history of increasing recognition of this difference and of the necessary diminution of Germany's special conflict with the East, which resulted from the gradual absorption of the Federal Republic in the economic,

political and military system of the West, as well as from the growing limitation of more general forms of conflict between East and West as a consequence of détente.[4]

The *Ostpolitik* of the Social Democratic and Liberal coalition in Bonn was only one aspect of Western policy towards Eastern Europe, taking its place within the wider framework of the comprehensive range of relations between the superpowers and their allies on both sides. In this respect *Ostpolitik* was not only an adaptation to change but also an attempt to explore and, if possible, to extend the range of options for West German foreign policy. The American political scientist Wolfram Hanrieder sees this as follows:

> Willy Brandt's greatest service was, through diplomacy and personal effort, to make a virtue out of the necessity in which the FRG found itself, of having to accept the status quo. In the same way it had been Adenauer's greatest contribution to make a virtue out of the need to find a constructive *modus vivendi* with the Western powers. Both were faced with the difficult task of directing German diplomacy, in response to unavoidable pressures, towards accepting the situation imposed by international developments, discarding some aspects of the German position, and making compromises. . . .
>
> However dynamic Brandt's *Ostpolitik* was in many respects, it consisted basically of a policy of resignation, designed less to create change in the immediate future than to prevent the chances of change in the longer term being removed.[5]

This left the way open for the introduction of a process of détente and normalisation throughout Europe. By May 1972, almost simultaneously with the Bundestag's ratification of the Eastern treaties, the countries of NATO and the Warsaw Pact decided to arrange a Conference on Security and Cooperation in Europe (CSCE). This Conference was not concerned primarily with solving the central problems arising from Europe's division between East and West; rather, it was to make it possible to achieve greater international security and stronger cooperation in a situation characterised by the fact that these problems were unsolved — and, in many cases, insoluble.

4. R. Löwenthal, 'Vom kalten Krieg zur Ostpolitik', in idem and H.-P. Schwarz (eds.), *Die zweite Republik. 25 Jahre Bundesrepublik Deutschland — eine Bilanz*, Stuttgart, 1974, pp. 604f.
5. W. Hanrieder, *Fragmente der Macht. Die Aussenpolitik der Bundesrepublik*, Munich, 1981, p. 82

*Final Act of the Conference on Security and Cooperation in Europe (CSCE), 1
August 1975 (Helsinki Final Act)*

The Helsinki Final Act can be seen as the cornerstone, at multi-
lateral level, of West Germany's *Ostpolitik*. The list of Principles in
the so-called 'Basket I' (questions relating to security in Europe)
essentially reproduces elements of the Eastern treaties, while not
standing in the way of peaceful change in Europe.

Principle I establishes 'sovereign equality' and 'respect for the
rights inherent in sovereignty', and also the recognition of the
participant states 'that their frontiers can be changed, in accordance
with international law, through peaceful means and by agreement'.
The most important case in which 'peaceful change' would occur is
with the realisation of the right to self-determination of peoples,
guaranteed under Principle VIII. According to this, 'all peoples
always have the right, in full freedom, to determine when and as
they wish, their internal and external political status, without external interference, and to pursue as they wish their political, economic, social and cultural development'.

Principle II ('Refraining from the threat or use of force') contains
a general prohibition on force, especially emphasising that the
'territorial integrity' and 'political independence' of any State should
be protected.

Principle III repeats, with minor differences of formulation, the
provisions of the Eastern treaties regarding the 'inviolability of
frontiers': the participating States 'regard as inviolable all one
another's frontiers as well as the frontiers of all States in Europe and
therefore they will refrain now and in the future from assaulting
these frontiers'.

Finally, Principle X contains a 'shall not affect' clause, in the
statement of the participants 'that the present Declaration does not
affect their rights and obligations, nor the corresponding treaties and
other agreements and arrangements'.

The Final Act, signed in Helsinki at the beginning of August 1975,
represents a declaration of common policy intent to create a system
of political and moral rules for the future behaviour of the thirty-five
signatory states (including the USA and Canada). Ten years after
Helsinki, the American diplomat John J. Maresca, deputy head of
the US delegation at the CSCE negotiations, took stock of progress:

The two most important aspects of the CSCE have generally been overlooked. The first is its historic role as a surrogate World War II peace treaty. A peace treaty of classic form is not possible in the present circumstances, since it would have to be signed with Germany, as one of the principal belligerents. Yet Germany is now divided into two countries, which could not by themselves sign a peace treaty underlining the fact that they really form one nation. By including the two Germanies in a much larger conference, it became possible to address the issues left from the war and to reach a conclusion that, accepted by all the belligerents, formally consigned the war to history.

The second point is the CSCE's role as a continuing European institution, now ten years old and still a dynamic enterprise. This institution is broad in scope and membership, flexible, and resistant to the moods of international relations. It has become a forum for debate and discussion between East and West, neutral and engaged, large countries and small, and has proven itself capable of positive contributions, even during periods of East–West tension. It has not been subverted to Soviet objectives — on the contrary, it has been used to advance many Western views — and its possibilities are far from exhausted. It seems clear that the CSCE has become a permanent part of the European landscape.[6]

The change in policy towards the East introduced by the SPD–FDP coalition in Bonn has remained the subject of political argument in West Germany. Its supporters point out that it enabled the Federal Republic at this time to free itself from the confrontation with the East of previous decades and to avoid international isolation. Europe's heartland was turned by détente from being a focus of the Cold War into a zone of comparative peace, making possible a more secure position for Berlin, contacts between the people of divided Germany, and a significant widening of economic relations with Eastern Europe. At the same time, the scope of West Germany's international relations was considerably extended.

Critics, on the other hand, take the view that the exaggerated expectations aroused by détente in the 1970s encouraged a playing-down of the evils of the Communist system and of Soviet power politics. With the establishment of its territorial status quo and its hegemony in Eastern and Central Europe, the Soviet Union achieved a remarkable success. While in the West détente led finally to a political and psychological loss of the will to maintain defence, the Soviet Union succeeded in extending its influence over Western Europe.

6. J.J. Maresca, *To Helsinki: The Conference on Security and Cooperation in Europe, 1973–1975*, Durham, NC, 1985, p. xii

Ten years after ratification of the West German treaties with the Eastern bloc, the following critical assessment was given by Alois Mertes, then Minister of State in the Bonn foreign office:

> A long-term consequence of détente has been the Western public's fluctuating consciousness of danger. Responsible leaders in the Western Alliance have always been aware of a dual risk to peace and freedom: the risk of nuclear self-destruction and the risk of Western Europe's insidious subordination of itself to the Soviet Union. Moscow wants a political victory from nuclear peace. It wants neither the risk of self-annihilation nor the destruction of Germany. Rather, the Soviet Union is striving to ward off trouble through its good behaviour, and thereby to increase the receptiveness of Western Europe — above all the non-nuclear Federal Republic — towards Moscow's efforts at political influence.[7]

The End of Détente?

The failure of East–West détente in the 1970s was dramatically underlined by the Soviet invasion of Afghanistan in the last month of the decade and by the events in Poland at the beginning of the 1980s. However, the real reasons lay in disruption by exogenous factors and in unexpected repercussions which in the preceding years had already weakened the détente process and in part even reversed it. At the same time, the differing effects of events in Afghanistan and Poland upon the process of détente in Europe illustrate the paradox of the détente era. Both its defeats and its successes, as also the extension and weakening of Soviet power, were harmful to the détente process, since they stimulated reactions in either West or East which first limited and then brought to an end the dynamic process of détente. The major reason must be seen in the fact that détente can only be described as successful if the premise of an equal balance of power is adhered to.

Even for the Soviet Union, the Helsinki accord soon became a mixed blessing. While contributing outwardly to the stabilisation of the Eastern bloc within the international system, Helsinki at the same time opened the way for internal relaxations. The strengthening of the position of hegemony over Eastern Europe desired by the Soviet Union thus went hand in hand with a weakening on the inside. The French expert on Eastern bloc affairs, Hélène Carrère

7. A. Mertes, 'Bilanz der Entspannungspolitik', in *Aus Politik und Zeitgeschichte*, 50, 1982, pp. 4ff.

d'Encausse, has described the effects of détente on the socialist camp:

> Détente, which initially led to an intensive dialogue between the two giants of world affairs, appears also to change fundamentally the relations between communist states and to make way for aspirations concerning national interests, economic development, the exchange of ideas and human rights. It is no accident that everywhere in the socialist countries Helsinki Committees have been formed. For the first time since 1945, forces for freedom within socialism believe in help from outside, and in the validity of principles which are above all political systems.[8]

A further source of the shift in power lies in the fact that during the 1970s a military imbalance developed which was in the Soviet Union's favour, although this applied less to the intercontinental strategic missiles which serve as mutual deterrence for both Soviet Union and USA, by virtually neutralising the opponent's weapons. Through their production and installation of the intermediate-range missiles, the SS–20s, the Soviets achieved a breakthrough which has given them the possibility of threatening all the areas bordering on their own sphere of control — from Western Europe, via the Middle East to China and Japan — without being exposed automatically to a reciprocal threat from the USA.

There thus became apparent a loophole in the deterrence strategy of flexible response, which led to the questioning of the credibility of a strategy supposed by military planners to ensure the preservation of peace. In 1977 the then Chancellor of the Federal Republic, Helmut Schmidt, was the first to point out this loophole, in a lecture given to the International Institute of Strategic Studies in London:

> But strategic arms limitation confined to the United States and the Soviet Union will inevitably impair the security of the West European members of the Alliance *vis-à-vis* Soviet military superiority in Europe if we do not succeed in removing the disparities of military power in Europe parallel to the SALT negotiations. So long as this is not the case we must maintain the balance of the full range of deterrence strategy. The Alliance must, therefore, be ready to make available the means to support its present strategy, which is still the right one, and to prevent any developments that could undermine the basis of this strategy.[9]

8. H. Carrere d'Encausse, 'Histoire d'un malentendu', in *Après la détente* (un dossier de la revue *politique internationale*), Paris, 1982, p. 17
9. H. Schmidt, 'The 1977 Alastair Buchan Memorial Lecture', in *Survival*, vol. XX, no. 1, January/February 1978, p. 4

With the so-called NATO twin-track decision of 12 December 1979 (see also p. 45) the Alliance decided after intensive public debate in member countries, particularly in the Federal Republic, to counter the Soviet capability with an intermediate-range missile system of its own, albeit limited in numbers. It was chiefly as a result of pressure from the Europeans that this decision was tied closely to an offer to negotiate an abstention from implementing the missile deployment if progress on arms control made this possible. In a much-quoted article in the newsmagazine *Die Zeit*, the physicist and philosopher Carl Friedrich von Weizsäcker warned of the dilemma posed for the West as a result of this decision:

> The new, land-based intermediate-range missiles cause (justifiable!) anxiety to the general public and it will become more and more difficult, in all the countries of Western Europe, to carry out their deployment against the resistance of the people for whose protection they are intended. But it is precisely these developments which place the governments of Western Europe, and especially our own government, in an almost insoluble dilemma, where they are forced into an unwelcome and unbearable choice between loyalty to their American allies and the needs of their own people for external security. The Alliance will be discredited among our people, if we carry out to the letter the decision on weapons modernisation, and we will be discredited among the American public, with its renewed militancy against the Soviet Union, if we try to get out of this decision. Now that this situation has arisen, the linking of the decision on nuclear missiles to the offer of disarmament negotiations serves little purpose. For in this situation the Soviet Union hardly needs to fear our determination to deploy armaments, and so it loses the motivation to accede to our demands to limit their own intermediate-range missiles. But the failure of 'Eurostrategic disarmament' would considerably increase the dangers to Europe in the precarious situation of the 1980s. An unhappy decision.[10]

The twin-track decision was intended primarily — besides its disarmament aspects — to establish a community of risk between America and Western Europe, which would exclude the option for the USA to pursue a limited war in Europe by making it militarily possible. It was this extension of risk, and the growing awareness of it, which led on both sides of the Atlantic to disquiet about the 1979 decision and about the Alliance itself. Those governments in Western Europe affected by missile deployment considered themselves

10. C.F.v. Weizsäcker, 'Die neuen Raketen gehören auf See', in *Die Zeit*, 22 May 1981

not to be in a position to give effect to the decision to station the planned medium-range missiles until they could plausibly argue that the West had indeed exhausted all other options. This question became especially critical because the Reagan Administration, which took office in 1981, left no doubts as to its negative attitude towards arms controls. As a result, fears were expressed, and not only by the opponents of missile modernisation, that all the Americans had to do was to allow negotiations to fail, to the accompaniment of dramatic gestures of good will.

In the United States, the Europeans were accused of cultivating the growth of a flourishing and — at least in part — anti-American-inspired peace movement, and of not being prepared to carry their fair share of the burdens of joint defence. To those European countries where the missiles would be stationed the NATO twin-track decision seemed, above all, to contain the threat that they could be drawn into a conflict which had broken out elsewhere and which might then be fought out in Europe. Public controversy soon concentrated on the issue of the morality of deterrence. Both church leaders and many lay people published a wide range of arguments to show that a strategy of mutual deterrence would be supported only on certain conditions and only for the next few years, at most.

Soviet and American Intermediate-range Missiles in Europe

In June 1987 the Soviet Union had more than 440 SS–20 missiles operational, with a range of up to 5,000 km and each carrying three warheads; it also had about 120 SS–4s with a range of 1,900 km and a single warhead. This meant that the number of warheads on Soviet land-based intermediate-range missiles had more than doubled since 1976, and more than quadrupled if one counted the total loading capacity of the SS–20s.

In compliance with the NATO twin-track decision of 1979 a total of 108 Pershing II missiles, with a range of up to 1,800 km and with only one warhead each, have been deployed in West Germany since November 1983. So far 208 Cruise missiles, each with a range of up to 2,500 km, have been stationed in Great Britain, Italy and the FRG, out of a projected total of 464.

The so-called Double-Zero Agreement now negotiated between the United States and the USSR would probably eliminate those missiles.

The Crisis of Credibility in the Atlantic Alliance

For the twelve years from the Harmel Report to the NATO twin-track decision of 1979, defence and détente remained in symbiotic relationship as the joint tasks of the Alliance. As most European governments have fallen in with the American course of stronger emphasis on the military component, conflict over the aims of the Alliance and individual national interests has certainly become less sharp at the present time. Yet even among the supporters of weapons modernisation there is some disquiet that the dynamic of the missile programme could lead in the long term to unacceptable risks to international security.

During the seventy-fifth meeting of the Bergedorfer Gesprächs-kreis in Moscow in June 1984, twelve German and twelve Russian participants discussed 'Problems of political and military détente' in the context of the future of Europe. Horst Teltschik, Chancellor Kohl's Security Adviser, analysed the conditions required for an improvement in East–West relations:

> The balance between East and West is too fragile for it to be able to remain confined to its military components. Today both sides have at their disposal a nuclear, conventional, and sea-borne weapons capability which could annihilate their opponents many times over. We must face up to the fact that the arms race has produced not more security for East and West, but less. The arms race itself has become a source of tension, uncertainty and mutual suspicion. Quite apart from the material costs which place burdens on our people which they are ever less willing to bear, both in the West and in the East. . . . It is high time, therefore, that the nuclear arsenal is drastically reduced.
>
> Both sides ought to be aware that mutual trust can only be reestablished if proof is given that some concrete agreements can be achieved, even if these appear insignificant. Both East and West have made enough declarations of intent. People are now waiting for practical solutions. At the moment no results are in prospect either in disarmament or arms control. But this situation would really become dangerous, if at the same time the political dialogue between the two superpowers came to a standstill.[11]

In reality, West Europeans perceive their opportunities of influencing global politics, even when these affect the position of Europe, as a great deal more limited now than even two

---

11. H. Teltschik, *Probleme der politischen und militärischen Entspannung*, Hamburg, 1984, pp. 12ff.

or three years ago. It has become harder to talk to, and reach agreement with, the American Administration since President Reagan gave priority to strengthening the global position of the USA by military means, and his concept of the USA's leadership role has allowed less and less room for consultation with its allies.

The consequence has been a crisis of confidence in current defence policies which, in Western Europe especially, has marked the whole climate of politics, affecting not only young people and a large part of the Left, but many other sections of society as well. In the light of the experience of the 1970s, when despite détente there was never any pause in the massive Soviet arms build-up, the Americans finally signalled their determination to replenish their own weapons capability in a significant measure, and the consensus on the basic problems of preserving peace has broken down even further.

Part of public opinion in Western Europe saw the worsening climate in international relations as largely, or almost exclusively, the fault of the USA. Many found it acceptable to justify Soviet policies as being based on their extremely high defence requirements once it became clear that Soviet policy took little account of West European defence needs. Remarkably, fear of the unchallengeable might of the Soviet Union did not develop into hostility towards the Soviets but rather into a loss of trust in the protective capacity of the Western alliance.

Professor Stanley Hoffmann of Harvard sees these reactions as a direct result of Western Europe's dependence on the USA for its defence, that is, for issues of life and death:

> Western Europe is a frying pan on a stove whose controls are in the hands of others. Irresponsibility and resentment are the inevitable outcomes. Nations which must rely on others for their defense, and consequently for much of their foreign policy, often tend to turn inward, leaving to those others the responsibility — and the blame — for difficult decisions. For many years now the architects of the European Community, trying to make a virtue of necessity, have argued that their new entity would be 'civilian' in nature, repudiating power politics and behaving as a model for others. Defense matters have been left to NATO, where key decisions are made unilaterally by the United States, or collectively at American initiative. As a result, Western Europe has had the worst of both worlds — the trials of a collective new political entity, without control over the one issue that stands at the heart of sovereignty and authority.[12]

12. S. Hoffmann, 'Nato and Nuclear Weapons: Reasons and Unreason', in *Foreign Affairs*, Winter 1981/2, p. 343

Europe's weakness encourages the trend towards bipolarity in global politics, and for questions affecting the fate of the entire world to be dealt with by Washington and Moscow alone. If the Europeans are to try to achieve multipolarity in the global political system, thus allowing them to defend their own interests with greater independence, they must first create, through mutual agreement and cooperation, a centre of gravity in Europe which will exert its own pull in world affairs. This would have to take place within the existing Western Alliance, which relies on the might of the USA and which would collapse if separated from a major world power. A study done in Vienna of the future prospects of Western defence policies comments:

> If Western Europe's defence policy were gradually to achieve greater autonomy, this could give life to the latent desire among West Europeans to assert themselves more forcefully; it could lessen the striking inequalities in burdens and responsibilities within the Alliance and thereby encourage consensus building both on internal and external policies. The continual demands of the Americans for the Europeans to take on a greater share of defence costs can politically only be acceded to if Western Europe's influence over the shaping of key NATO policy guidelines on defence increases, and if this explicitly involves American nuclear strategy.
>
> If the European wish to assert their viewpoint is to become more credible, then they will have to be able to show readiness for defensive action and sacrifice in other ways than through the threat of nuclear retaliation. A defence policy which requires the people in the front line to be prepared for nuclear suicide is not a sound basis from which to develop either the healthy expression of independent views, or external security policies for the West which are arrived at by consensus.[13]

International developments since the sudden drop in the global political temperature at the end of the last decade have not only led to a great public controversy over basic questions of the prevention of war and on international security; a second area of differences in opinion between the USA and its allies lies in the question of how to judge the effects of East–West economic relations on national security in the widest sense.

In the détente period of the 1970s economic exchanges were encouraged, in line with the Harmel formula of 1967, with the aim of developing a network of relations which the Soviet bloc, too, would be interested in maintaining and which neither side could have

---

13. K.E. Birnbaum, 'Friedenssicherung, atomare Bedrohung und öffentliche Meinung', in *Europa-Archiv*, 3, 1984, p. 77

destroyed without damaging important interests of its own. In opposition to this was the Reagan Administration's thesis that the refusal of economic cooperation was more likely to contribute to a greater restraint in Soviet foreign policy, a reduction in their arms expenditure, and the emergence of a readiness for internal reform.

When, after the Soviet invasion of Afghanistan and the imposition of martial law in Poland, the USA advocated a policy of economic sanctions, the countries of Western Europe rejected the idea of the usefulness of economic pressure as a means of changing Soviet behaviour. Unlike the American Administration many Europeans do not see trade with the East as a risk to security, but rather regard these exchanges as mutually advantageous. At a meeting of experts on East–West economic relations, Heinrich Vogel, director of the Cologne-based Federal Institute for Eastern and International Studies, said:

> One of the less commonly cited versions of the famous Murphy's Law, which like the original is marked by bitter experience and an air of resignation, runs as follows: 'People and nations tend to begin behaving rationally only when all other possibilities have been exhausted'. One is tempted to elevate this formulation to a General Law of East–West Relations. The mistrust which is now rife, the technique of mutual recrimination, the search for points of vulnerability, and the labelling of all kinds of 'traps' (the credit trap, the high-technology trap) into which people were enticed by their respective partners from the other side in the course of détente, all this has taken on grotesque forms in the area of economic relations between East and West.
>
> It is, finally, in the nature of things that economic relations are only ever developed if they serve the advantage of both sides. Nothing will change the fact that they also contain a risk of political misuse which becomes all the greater, as mutual trust in the capacity and readiness of the partners to preserve these relations becomes less clear.[14]

Differing concepts of their responsibility and correspondingly different expectations were at the origin of not inconsiderable divergences between the American and the European assessments of the possible function and conceptual value of détente. Whereas the Western superpower's policies towards the East tended towards a strategy of holding back, the Europeans claimed that under conditions of a

14. H. Vogel, 'Vertrauensförderung durch alle Beteiligten notwendig', discussion paper from an East Berlin Academic Symposium on East–West Economic Relations: The present Political and Economic Environment, 24–26 March 1983, in *Wissenschaft und Frieden*, 3–4, 1983, p. 129

perfect power balance, continual political efforts are necessary in order to reduce, step by step, the antagonism between the two systems. In parallel with the worsening of relations between the superpowers, there also occurred a reduction in readiness to achieve even a partial accommodation between Eastern and Western interests in Europe. The realisation of this fact creates growing insecurity — especially in Central Europe, on the most heavily-armed front between the two political camps. The problems arising in the future from these differing ways of seeing the relationship between East and West were analysed by an expert from America:

> One basic issue is how to explain the rise and demise of détente in the 1970s and whether to continue to seek dialogue with the Soviet Union in the future. The Reagan Administration is critical of the concept of détente and sceptical about the possibility of achieving durable results on a range of issues through cooperative dialogue with the Soviet Union. As seen by this Administration, the Soviet leaders violated the rules of détente in the 1970s through their expansionist policy in the third world and they betrayed what was seen as a mutually agreed-upon code of conduct to exercise global restraint. Moreover, they increased their military forces while the United States did not. In global terms, therefore, the Soviet Union did not abide by its commitments, as defined in the United States.
>
> The Europeans had more limited, regional expectations of détente. They tend to judge Soviet conduct by how the Kremlin behaves in Europe, as opposed to the rest of the world. Their view is that despite the deployment of Soviet SS–20 missiles, Moscow has behaved with relative restraint towards Europe, even though it may have broken an American-defined set of rules. The Europeans, because of their greater proximity to the Soviet Union, tend to be more conscious than the United States of the effects of the Second World War on the Soviet Union, and are consequently more liable to accept the legitimacy of Soviet insecurities. Because of these different evaluations of Soviet conduct, Western Europe is more favourably disposed than the United States towards seeking a dialogue with the Russians on a variety of issues and believes that agreements with Moscow are feasible.[15]

Since the end of 1984 the militant rhetoric of the Reagan Administration has noticeably softened in tone. In the election campaign, the American President even raised the efforts at achieving arms control to the level of a priority for his second term of office, and

15. A.E. Stent, 'East–West Trade and Technology Transfer: the West's Search for Consensus', in *The World Today*, November 1984, pp. 453–4

thereby smoothed the way for the most complex round of talks in the history of American–Soviet arms control negotiations. The new Soviet leadership under Mikhail Gorbachev, in office since March 1985, is also interested in a respite. However, the main Soviet effort appears to be concentrated on getting an agreement that would end in a denuclearisation of Western Europe and a world beyond nuclear deterrence. What the Europeans fear is a 'decoupling' of US nuclear deterrence from European defences. They are also worried that the so-called Double-Zero Option, providing for the removal of medium-range and short-range missiles, would be too large a step toward eliminating nuclear weapons. Moreover, they believe nuclear weapons are needed as a deterrent in view of Warsaw Pact superiority in conventional forces.

The meeting between Reagan and Gorbachev in Washington in December 1987 and the signing of the agreement to scrap intermediate-range nuclear weapons has, paradoxically perhaps, both clarified and confused the situation. On the one hand, at superpower level, Murphy's Law, as defined above by Vogel, came into force: the irrationalities and unacceptable costs of the escalating superpower arms race had become all too clear and brought the two sides together. Further breakthroughs may now be possible. On the other hand, from the European perspective, the accord has merely exacerbated the above-mentioned European insecurities. They see the desirability of reducing tensions, but they are also concerned to preserve specific regional interests. Above all, in search of the ideal road they find themselves torn between the 'Atlanticists', who continue to accept the lead of the hegemonic power, and those who think of constructing a more or less independent European position within the Atlantic Alliance. Almost inevitably, these divergences are particularly acute in West Germany, as they have been in the past.

3 / The Two Germanies and East–West Relations

Through their membership of two very different alliances the two German states both focus on and give expression to the comprehensive range of differences existing between East and West. Already in the late 1940s, and increasingly in the two decades which followed, it was evident that the Germans were among those who suffered most from Soviet–American confrontations. The Berlin Blockade of 1948–9, Nikita Khrushchev's Berlin Ultimatum of 1958, the building of the Berlin Wall in August 1961, all fell hardest on the people living in these two countries; every renewal of East–West tensions in these years seriously affected the situation in Germany.

On the other hand, improvements in the climate of relations between Washington and Moscow helped to make life in divided Germany easier. In 1963, following the Cuban crisis, it became possible for agreements to be reached by Bonn and East Berlin on travel visas for Berliners divided by the Wall. Again, after 1969, as détente facilitated a range of international agreements, it was the Germans who benefited most from these and particularly from the Quadripartite Agreement on Berlin and the Treaty on the Bases of Relations and its subsidiary agreements, as worked out between Bonn and East Berlin.

Throughout the whole postwar period, at least until the end of the 1960s, the political freedom of action for both German states proved to be dependent almost entirely upon the current state of East–West relations. Neither Bonn nor East Berlin could pursue their own efforts if these ran counter to the current trend in those relations. Only in the 1980s is there a trend in the relations between the two Germanies which appears to run counter to international relations generally, thus indicating a gradual widening of scope and greater flexibility in their mutual relations.

Because of the deteriorating political climate after the Russian invasion of Afghanistan and the missile deployment strategies of the two superpowers, there were signs that brother Germans in the opposing camps were ready to pursue détente and to continue their former course towards at least partial understanding. Until the cancellation of Honecker's visit to the Federal Republic, in September 1984, the GDR maintained its contacts with Bonn despite the obvious open disapproval of Moscow. Even after this, East Berlin let it be known that it does not want to break off the contacts built up with Bonn — at least not on those matters already under discussion.

When in the autumn of 1982 the CDU/CSU again became the main party of government after thirteen years of SPD/FDP coalitions, there were new approaches in several areas but, to the surprise of many people, policy on Germany was spared from fundamental change. If we bear in mind the fact that the majority of the CDU/CSU parliamentary party has continued to be rather reserved on the Eastern and inner-German treaties of the Brandt-Scheel era, the attitude of Chancellor Kohl signifies a change for his own party and an astonishing degree of continuity as regards the *Deutschlandpolitik* of his Social Democratic-Liberal predecessors in government. Even in the more difficult international conditions of recent years, the new government in Bonn has succeeded in getting improvements in the practical approach and general attitude of the East German authorities towards frontier controls, and to obtain what for a while was an extraordinarily generous way of handling applications for travel to the West. At the same time, by offering the East German leadership sizeable credits, guaranteed by West German banks, as well as easing payment requirements in inner-German trade, the Federal Republic has signalled its readiness to honour the concessions made on humanitarian questions.

The Shifting Limits on Freedom of Action in Times of Crisis

The emergence of a 'mini-détente' between the Germanies during a period of sharpened confrontation between the two leaders of their respective alliances raised for the first time the question as to whether it is possible for the relationship between the two German states to develop quite independently of the overall international situation. Given the inflexible attitudes of the two superpowers, demands were increasingly heard that the Germans should sound out the scope for negotiation on their own and without necessarily being tied to their respective alliances.

Here it is worth quoting the view of one Bonn diplomat on the chances of an independent foreign policy for the two German states emerging in the 1980s:

The political freedom of action for the GDR in times of crisis has, in my opinion, only developed beyond those of previous years and decades, to the extent that Moscow now permits its German ally to make more original contributions of its own to the implementation of an otherwise common policy, already agreed down to the details. Any tendency towards an equidistant stance in relation to the two superpowers, as advocated at the present time in some political circles in the Federal Republic, is not discernible in the GDR.

Without doubt, the FRG's position in the Western Alliance is something quite different from that of the GDR in its alliance. The very different political system throughout NATO, the democratic element in the Atlantic Community, place limits on the dominance of its superpower and leader, the USA. . . . The room for manoeuvre which the Federal Republic has in times of international tension is certainly a lot greater than that of the GDR, albeit still clearly limited. Even so, it has in the past usually been sufficient to allow West Germany in a few instances to promote its own specific interests.[1]

In a lecture at a German–American seminar held by the Konrad Adenauer Foundation in Washington, the then Bonn Minister for Inner-German Relations, Heinrich Windelen, made clear the reasons why the Federal Republic ought to be interested in a widening in scope of East Germany's relations, also:

We are not interested in harming the GDR or destabilising it. What we do want is to reach practical solutions, and for that the GDR needs just as much room for manoeuvre as we do ourselves. For this reason we base our stand on the facts of the situation, which in terms of power politics are quite clear. So we see our responsibility as Germans and Europeans as being to do what is possible and responsible today, in order to limit as far as we can East–West conflict in Germany and Europe, and to ensure the likelihood of change in the future.[2]

The American Jonathan Dean, a diplomat who knows Germany well, takes the view that it is precisely in times of crisis that Bonn's *Deutschlandpolitik* offers the United States more advantages than disadvantages:

1. W. Schollwer, 'Der politische Handlungsspielraum der Bundesrepublik und der DDR im Zeichen internationaler Spannungen', in *Liberal*, July/August 1981, pp. 484ff.
2. H. Windelen, 'Die Grundfragen der Deutschlandpolitik der Bundesregierung', conference at a German-American Seminar of the Konrad Adenauer Foundation, Washington, 7 February 1984, in *Bulletin. Presse- und Informationsamt der Bundesregierung*, 15, 1984, pp. 133ff.

The Federal Republic's policy towards East Germany has some very solid benefits for the United States that are not of purely regional significance: it reduces tension between the two German states in the area of the world's largest military confrontation; it promotes continued Soviet and East German restraint on West Berlin; and it stabilizes East Germany. . . . The Americans should consider this activity a constructive and practical West German contribution to Western policy toward the Soviet Union, a kind of political burden sharing. . . .

The Federal Republic will not return to its 1950s policy of providing almost automatic support to the United States on East–West issues. Bonn's Eastern policy has established new West German interests and relationships that will not be abandoned and that limit its ability to give the United States automatic or enthusiastic support on any position it may take in East–West issues. By any measure, however, the compensating gain far outweighs this loss.[3]

After the start of American missile deployment on West German soil in November 1983, informed public opinion was at first expecting a particularly difficult period in relations between the two Germanies. At any rate Honecker himself, shortly before the NATO weapons modernisation plan was put into effect, had warned of a new 'Ice Age' in relations between the GDR and the FRG, consistent with the picture sketched by the then Soviet party chief, Yuri Andropov: after the missile-stationing, the citizens of the two German states could be looking at each other through a stockade of missiles.

However, the GDR conducted a surprisingly public debate with the Soviet Union, disregarding all such dire prophecies, and repeatedly stressing the particular concern of all Germans for the preservation of peace, and hence their special responsibilities for relations between the two German states. In a speech before the 7th Plenum of the Central Committee of the SED (East German Communist Party) at the end of November 1983, Honecker, disregarding the political implications, argued for a continuation of the dialogue between the two German states, and at the same time revealed the limits on his own freedom of action:

We cannot overlook the fact that through this decision [on missile deployment] the whole system of European treaties, including the Treaty on the Bases of Relations between the GDR and the FRG, has suffered serious damage. We are for the limitation of this damage as far as possible. . . . So that no one may have any illusions, let it be said once more that we must hold onto the facts of the situation which results from

3. J. Dean, 'How to Lose Germany', in *Foreign Policy*, 55, Summer 1984, pp. 70f.

the Second World War and the immediate postwar period. That is the only basis on which to proceed. The GDR, as the first socialist state of workers and farmers on German soil, is firmly anchored in the Warsaw Pact and indissolubly allied to the Soviet Union. It is ready at all times to fulfil its alliance obligations.[4]

Characteristically, the expression 'damage limitation' met with considerable opposition in Moscow. In the context of a broad press campaign, understood everywhere as representing serious criticism of the GDR's policy towards the Federal Republic, *Pravda* described such an attitude as hypocritical, though without associating this term with Honecker personally:

> Typically, they are trying in Bonn to base their current massive pressure upon the GDR on a kind of special mission of the two German states to 'limit the damage' caused by the newest round of the arms race in Europe. Truly this is the logic of hypocrisy! In the first place, the ruling circles in the FRG gave a boost to this arms race, along with the USA and their other partners in NATO, by stationing the American missiles, and thereby doing enormous harm to the process of détente and relations between socialist and capitalist countries. Now, under the pretext of 'damage limitation', they are trying to carry out their old revanchist plans, which will certainly make the situation in Europe even more complicated.[5]

The GDR and its Eastern Allies

In this way, the Soviet Union let it be understood that the general lines of global policy for the Eastern bloc were laid down by the USSR and that the key to solving the German problem lay, as before, with Moscow. In the Soviet view, the need for this clarification arose also because the GDR was not alone among Warsaw Pact countries in expressing openly its own interest in relaxing tensions in East–West relations. This position is shared with Hungary and Romania, who also refer to the responsibility of all European countries, irrespective of their size, for the future development of the Continent.

More recently, as a result of the CSCE process, the smaller countries of Eastern Europe have begun increasingly to put forward

---

4. E. Honecker, 'Diskussion auf der 7. Plenarsitzung des ZK der SED' in East Berlin, 25 November 1983, in *Neues Deutschland*, 26–7 November 1983
5. *Pravda*, 2 August 1984

their own interests, which are frequently in conflict with their supranational commitments as alliance members. In a noteworthy article, Mátyás Szürös, head of the foreign policy section of the Central Committee of the Hungarian Socialist Workers' Party, has explained the relationship between the national and the supranational in the socialist community, in terms with which the SED did largely agree:

> The lessons of our troubled history, our geographical position and our current circumstances all make us aware that we can only achieve the goals of building up our society and economy in an international situation of peace and security, and through making best use of the opportunities offered by extensive and mutually advantageous relations with countries whose social orders differ from our own. We are therefore convinced supporters of dialogue, of practical negotiations, and fair deals. . . . Only such an interpretation of common goals can meet today's requirements, in the current phase of socialist development: an interpretation which takes account of the fundamental national interests of cooperating countries, and of efforts directed towards creating the necessary international conditions for asserting those interests.[6]

What these carefully-worded phrases make clear is that strict limitations on cooperation between East and West in Europe would affect the smaller countries of Eastern Europe to a disproportionately greater extent than their superpower ally. This is also the background to the GDR's efforts, not only to define its role in the Warsaw Pact as a front line state between two antagonistic social orders, but to describe itself and to offer itself as a partner in a process of détente embracing both political systems. Unlike Hungary and Romania, however, even in the 1980s the GDR is still the state with the greatest limitations on its sovereignty within the Soviet ambit.

As a country whose origins lie in the German defeat of 1945, the GDR sees itself in a less favourable legal position than other Warsaw Pact states. East Germany places all its armed forces, without exception, at the Warsaw Pact's disposal, leading to a very close intermeshing of its troops with the Soviet armed forces. The East German defence ministry has an unusually large staff and to all appearances, unlike the other partners in the Pact, must submit to foreign decision-making in fulfilling all aspects of its support duties. Whereas all non-German versions of the Warsaw Pact treaty of 14

---

6. M. Szürös, 'Gemeinsame Ziele, nationale Interessen', repr. in *Neues Deutschland*, 12 April 1984

May 1955 lay down that each participant state has to afford its allies the assistance which 'it' considers necessary, in the German version it is assistance which 'they' consider necessary that is required. On the basis of its 1957 treaty with the GDR on the stationing of troops, the USSR claims for its total of 400,000 men on East German territory a quasi-sovereign immunity, with no limitations on their ability to intervene in East German internal affairs. To the present day the Soviet Union lays stress on its political responsibilities for the whole of Germany and in the Quadripartite Agreement on Berlin of 1971 it once again recognised the rights and responsibilities of the Four Powers.

Warsaw Pact Treaty of 14 May 1955 (translation of extract from the German version)

Art. 4: In the event of an armed attack in Europe on one or more of the States Parties to the Treaty by any State or group of States, each State of the Treaty shall, in the exercise of the right of individual or collective self-defence, in accordance with Art. 51 of the United Nations Charter, afford the State or States so attacked immediate assistance, individually and in agreement with the other States Parties to the Treaty, by all means they consider necessary, including the use of armed force.

The peculiar position of the GDR within the Eastern power bloc is even secured in constitutional law. East Germany is the only country in the world which in its constitution has allied itself 'irrevocably' with the Soviet Union and declared itself an inseparable and component part of the socialist community of states. At the same time, it is also the only state within its alliance which lacks an independent national identity within the confines of its own frontiers.

Constitution of the German Democratic Republic of 9 April 1968 amended 7 October 1974 (extract)

Art. 6(2): The German Democratic Republic is allied for ever and irrevocably with the Union of Socialist Soviet Republics. The close and brotherly alliance with it guarantees the people of the German Democratic Republic further progress on the path of socialism and of peace.

The German Democratic Republic is an inseparable component part of the socialist community of states. It contributes, true to the principles of socialist internationalism, to its strengthening, fosters and develops friendship, mutual collaboration, and mutual aid with all states of the socialist community.

From this dual focus on the Eastern bloc and on the Federal Republic, which the majority of the population does not regard as a foreign country, an ambivalent policy results. In the mid-1970s Peter Christian Ludz, a West German expert on the GDR, wrote of GDR policy goals:

> The SED leadership has always had to pursue a range of different goals, which to the West may appear conflicting, and which are certainly not easily combined. They aim at separation from the outside world, above all from the Federal Republic, while signalling the simultaneously existing desire to build up economic and technical cooperation. They state verbally, at least, the aim of integration in the Eastern bloc, while also, after Helsinki, seeking to keep open certain wider foreign policy options in the whole of Europe. They have to build a new 'image' for themselves towards the rest of the world as a peace-loving country, ready for integration and cooperation, and for their own people the image of an independent, sovereign state with equal rights in relation both to the Eastern bloc and to the Federal Republic.[7]

The GDR's essential dependence on the Soviet Union has not been altered by the developments in East–West relations of recent years. However, since the early 1980s there have been signs of an attitude gaining ground which seeks to combine the irrevocable loyalty to the East with a policy of détente. East Germany's relations with the Federal Republic are an important part, but not the sole content of this cautious change of direction, which is constantly being secured both internally and externally. Following the cancellation of Honecker's visit to the FRG in September 1984, the GDR has consistently pursued its diplomatic efforts to improve relations with the countries of Western Europe and has tried, under the slogan of 'securing peace' to contribute to the creation of a more tension-free atmosphere, at least in Europe. Peter Bender, a Berlin-based journalist, sees the GDR's changed perception of its role among its

7. P.C. Ludz, *Die DDR zwischen Ost und West. Politische Analysen 1961 bis 1976*, Munich, 1977, p. 249

Eastern allies as follows:

> Anyone looking at the GDR at the end of the 1960s would have seen a
> country placed geographically in the middle of Europe, yet sharing
> nothing of European attitudes. . . . Today in East Berlin, too, people
> argue in European terms, even if to a far lesser extent than in neighbour-
> ing capitals. The GDR has always had trouble, and its representatives
> always find it difficult, internally and externally, to gain a foothold in
> Western Europe and North America. But there is no longer the fortress
> complex, and the GDR wants, like others, to be a European country too,
> even if a socialist one.[8]

The Federal Republic and its Western Allies

Unlike the GDR, the Federal Republic was never subjected unilaterally and exclusively to a single occupying power. Thanks to the
presence and role in the occupation of its allies Great Britain and
France, American domination was mitigated, limited, and by no
means always unchallenged. There was never a treaty of mutual
assistance and friendship between Bonn and Washington of the kind
which the Soviet Union has signed and regularly renewed with its
East European allies. Well before joining NATO, the FRG found
itself firmly embedded in a West European Community which has
enough weight and pull of its own to provide a counter-weight to the
leading power in the West.

The Federal Republic of Germany, through belonging to a variety
of organisations — the Atlantic Alliance, the European Community
and the West European Union — is part of an international network
covering all the major aspects of life. It not only has the largest
conventional armed forces but, after the United States, the FRG has
grown into the strongest country in the Atlantic community in terms
of its population and its economy. With other non-nuclear states it
shares Europe's fate, a loss of power. In the area of defence, at least,
Europe, far from shaping independent policies, is the object of
calculations of strategic balance which the superpowers reserve to
themselves.

In the 1980s this structural problem of the Atlantic Alliance has
become one of the most widely-discussed issues in Western defence
policy. Even if there has never been a credible alternative to strategic dependence on the United States, some Germans see their

8. P. Bender, 'Interessen in Mitteleuropa', in *Merkur*, 8, 1983, p. 868

security as increasingly threatened by their involvement in the system of mutual deterrence and the state of superpower relations. The inclination to gain greater security by distancing themselves from both sides has a polarising effect, without creating any greater freedom of action. In this situation, the old demands of the 1960s for a strengthening of the status and influence of European elements in the Alliance are gaining new currency. Gerd Ruge, then Editor-in-Chief, Television, of West German Radio (WDR), has assessed the chances for greater European autonomy within NATO:

> At the present time there is no model of a European or German defence strategy other than that of NATO which could credibly and reliably deter an attack or the threat of war; no such strategy can be developed without the USA or in opposition to it. It makes no difference whether one thinks purely of conventional defence or if the idea is more centred on civil defence or guerrilla warfare — in the situation of tension between the superpowers neither of these would prevent the use of nuclear war as a last resort, nor withstand determined conventional armed forces.
>
> All the same, there is the possibility of a role for Europe somewhere between the two poles of Washington and Moscow, which preserves ties to America as a counter-weight to the might of the Soviet Union, but without Europe being bound into the partnership with America against its will. The ideas behind such a policy should be worked out urgently. Then there could be a stronger and more independent European component in common defence policy, if Europeans are prepared to make a greater contribution on their own account. With a fresh division of contributions and responsibilities, greater equality could emerge within NATO's military leadership as between the USA and Western Europe, which might look less threatening to the Soviet Union, but would still provide a sufficient deterrent.[9]

It is surely no accident that in France, which has an independent defence policy, the national consensus on the need for the defence effort seems still unbroken, at least for the time being. Arguments that the Germans should have greater autonomy within a European framework, with explicit references to the Gaullist model, have been advanced by Karl Kaiser, an expert on defence matters and Director of the Research Institute of the German Foreign Policy Association in Bonn:

> Defence policy will have popular legitimacy if those whom it protects can feel that they have some influence on the central decisions affecting

---

9. G. Ruge, *Zwischen Washington und Moskau. Europa in der Konfrontation der Supermächte*, Frankfurt a.Main, 1984, p. 190

defence policy, that is, that their voice still counts. In de Gaulle's time, the French drew the conclusion that only the retention of decision-making at a purely national level could confer legitimacy on defence policies. The Federal Republic and other NATO partners, for reasons well known, were unable to give effect to such a conclusion themselves. Nevertheless, it is worth giving some consideration to the often-repeated French claim that the ability to make their own decisions is one reason for the high degree of national support and consensus for French defence policies.

However, because of the strategic defence position in Europe, decision-making autonomy can be strengthened only within a European framework, rather than at national level. For this reason the European Community offers new opportunities to strengthen the consensus on international security and to mobilise public support within Western Europe.[10]

The Federal Republic, because of its strategic position in Europe's heartland, could not withdraw from the Western Alliance without upsetting the balance, in unforeseen ways, in an area important in world politics. Moreover, the FRG's membership of the Western Alliance was from the beginning intended to achieve another, unspoken, but none the less real, purpose, that of serving simultaneously to control and to contain Germany. Pierre Hassner, a French expert on strategy, has described the historical background to this:

> Traditionally, the American attitude has been in close harmony with that of Konrad Adenauer: distrust of Germany's possible future evolution should lead it to being solidly integrated in a wider Western European and/or Atlantic whole: hence an attitude of embracing it in order to control it, both bilaterally and multilaterally. Germany, on the one hand being the most faithful and exposed ally today but potentially the least predictable and most dangerous tomorrow, was given a privileged voice on all American policies in Europe; on the other hand, collective structures were invented to preempt potential German demands, which, if and when they arose in the future, might lead to nationalist adventures, and to give them partial satisfaction within integrated structures. . . .[11]

The 1954 Paris Agreements between the Federal Republic and its

10. K. Kaiser, 'Politik für Europas Sicherheit. Ziele, Möglichkeiten und Probleme', in *Pro Pace. Beiträge und Analysen zur Sicherheitspolitik. Deutsches Strategie-Forum*, Bonn, 1984, p. 27
11. P. Hassner, 'The American World Power and the Western European Powers', in K. Kaiser and H.-P. Schwarz (eds.), *America and Western Europe, Problems and Prospects*, Lexington, 1977, p. 337

Western allies sealed the FRG's integration by international treaty in the Western system of alliances, while at the same time laying down guarantees which were intended to prevent the possibility of a Communist or neutral united Germany in the future. The Federal Republic was granted 'the full authority of a sovereign state', yet the special rights and responsibilities of the three Western powers 'in relation to Berlin and to Germany as a whole including the reunification of Germany and a peace settlement' were fully retained. The political reservations of the signatories lay in the setting of the goal of a reunited Germany which would have to have 'a liberal–democratic constitution' and be 'integrated within the European community'.

Convention on Relations Between the Three Powers and the Federal Republic of Germany (Germany Treaty), as amended 23 October 1954 (extract)

Art. 1(2): The Federal Republic shall have accordingly the full authority of a sovereign state over its internal and external affairs.

Art. 2: In view of the international situation, which has so far prevented the reunification of Germany and the conclusion of a peace settlement, the Three Powers retain the rights and the responsibilities, heretofore exercised or held by them, relating to Berlin and to Germany as a whole, including the reunification of Germany and a peace settlement.

Art. 7(2): Pending the peace settlement, the Signatory States will cooperate to achieve, by peaceful means, their common aim of a reunified Germany enjoying a liberal–democratic constitution, like that of the Federal Republic, and integrated within the European community.

The simultaneous accession of the Federal Republic to the North Atlantic Treaty and to the West European Union set the seal on the basic direction of Bonn's foreign policy, which within a few years received full support from all the major parties in the Bundestag, and from the SPD Opposition in 1960. The West European Union, which developed out of the Brussels Treaty of 1948, was modified and completed by protocol in 1954; it is significant principally because it commits the seven member states (Great Britain, France, the three Benelux countries, West Germany and Italy) to give each other automatic assistance, thus going further than the much vaguer NATO treaty. This advantage is nevertheless restricted by the fact

that the WEU as an organisation has no military planning organisation and would thus not be in a position either to plan or to carry out
joint action by the forces of its member states.

**Mutual Assistance Clauses in the North Atlantic Treaty (4 April 1949)
and the WEU Treaty (Amendment of 23 October 1954 to Brussels
Treaty)**

Art. 5 (North Atlantic Treaty): The parties agree that an armed attack
against one or more of them in Europe or North America shall be considered an attack against them all, and consequently agree that, if such an
armed attack occurs, each of them, in exercise of the right of individual or
collective self-defence recognized by Art. 51 of the UN Charter, will assist
the party or parties so attacked by taking forthwith, individually and in
concert with the other parties, such action as it deems necessary, including
the use of armed force, to restore and maintain the security of the North
Atlantic area.

Art. 5 (WEU Treaty): If any of the High Contracting Parties should be
the object of an armed attack in Europe, the other High Contracting Parties
will, in accordance with the provisions of Article 51 of the Charter of the
United Nations, afford the Party so attacked all the military and other aid
and assistance in their power.

The North Atlantic Treaty commits Germany to maintain a certain
minimum number of troops (12 divisions with a strength originally
set at 500,000 men); the WEU set an upper limit on this and
organised the control of German armaments until all restrictions
were abolished in 1983. At the time when it joined the WEU West
Germany had unilaterally renounced the production of atomic,
biological and chemical weapons (known as ABC weapons) on its
territory. It was the only member of NATO to have placed its entire
armed forces under integrated command in peacetime. On West
German territory are stationed troop contingents from six NATO
countries with a total strength of about 383,000 men. These factors
have a decisive influence on the range of options open for West
German defence policy.

There is no doubt that the crisis in East–West relations following
the invasion of Afghanistan sharpened awareness of these facts and
their consequences. The discussion on national security issues of the
last few years has shown that for at least part of the German

**Foreign troops stationed
in the two German states**

	United States 233,800	
	Great Britain 65,300	
	France 48,500	Soviet Union
	Belgium 25,000	
	Netherlands 5,500	
Total 383,100	Canada 5,000	Total 400,000

*Source: Facts and Figures: A Comparative Survey of the Federal Republic of Germany
and the German Democratic Republic, Bonn, 1986, p. 26.*

political, or rather intellectual, spectrum there is an increased
fascination with the idea of conducting foreign policy on primarily
national lines. The demands which emerged for greater sovereignty
for the Federal Republic have survived the missile debate which
originally gave rise to them. The thesis that the Germans are to a
large extent the victims of a conspiracy on the part of the United
States, or the Soviet Union, or both (according to viewpoint) has
become a favourite theme of many recent books on the 'national
question', which usually list the same few authors as contributors.
*The Left and the National Question, German Unity Must Come, No Future
without Germany, Inferiority as The Rationale of a State* — these are all
titles of books appearing between 1981 and 1985, which despite
differing political viewpoints have one thing in common: the demand
that the FRG leave the present alliance system.

It is of course highly questionable, whether West German chances
of controlling any conflict would be improved within a Europe
which, lacking the specific military integration in NATO, would not
carry the same weight within the power structure. As one study of
the Federal Republic's participation in the NATO decision-making
process put it in 1973:

It is most important to keep in mind that the Federal Republic of
Germany, with its exposed position in international politics, is so caught
up in the confrontation between two superpowers with antagonistic world
views, that even without the Alliance, the country would still belong among
those nations whose destinies it now links. Anyone realising the full implications of this will no longer see the possible limitations of Germany's
participation in conflict control by NATO as arising from arbitrarily-
evolved decision-making procedures, but rather from this historic

interdependence. With this assessment, the questionable procedures for decision-making on defence matters appear rightly in a new light: not as a diminution of sovereignty, but as an attempt to limit a loss of sovereignty which is inherent in the NATO structure, and to make it more calculable.[12]

Arguments of this kind are certainly plausible but do not alter the fundamental dilemma which characterises the exercise of national sovereignty in the nuclear age. In November 1983 Alexander Kluge, lawyer and film-maker, spoke on this issue at a public discussion in Munich:

> Sovereignty is derived from the questions: What would I risk my life for? What is my life worth to me? . . . The facts of our situation are that we could not offer ourselves, we would not even be asked, we would be committed to war against our will. If I want to safeguard and defend what is dearest to me — my child that looks to me in trust and believes in me, confident that I will soon find a way out, that I am big enough — then I come up against a terrible difficulty, because I know that neither I, nor anyone else sitting here, will be able to take the decision, because we simply won't be asked. We will be committed against our will, which is why it is so urgent to find out the truth of the situation. There must be some organisation, some community, some container, laboratory or factory in our society — it doesn't matter what we call it — that could produce the right combination of good-will, with the intensity and the urgency required (and, if necessary, even the ill-will too) to be able to keep the peace if it came to the crunch, and to defend what I value with my life.[13]

The Community of Responsibility Between the Two Germanies

The desire for peace, as old as humanity, becomes a factor making for strife, danger and instability in the nuclear age and in the context of East–West confrontation. There is no disputing that peace is the goal. What *is* in dispute is what that peace should look like and how it can be arrived at. In the Northern hemisphere, the freezing of international boundaries around the division of Germany and the split between two political systems gives both the Federal Republic

12. W. Hofmann, 'Die Beteiligung der Bundesrepublik Deutschland an den Entscheidungsprozessen der NATO', in *Regionale Verflechtung der Bundesrepublik Deutschland. Empirische Analysen und theoretische Probleme*, Munich/Vienna, 1973, p. 164
13. A. Kluge et al., *Reden über das eigene Land: Deutschland*, Munich, 1983, p. 90

and the GDR special roles in ensuring peace and security under the ever-present threat of international conflict.

Since the early 1970s this special role shared by the Germans in Europe has often been described by the expression 'community of responsibility'. The historian Rudolf von Thadden of Göttingen University, in a hearing before the Bundestag Committee for Inner-German Relations in 1981, referred the Germans of both states to the origins of their division and to their responsibility for its consequences:

> An effort to create a sense of German history today ought to start, in all honesty, from the fact that the Germans are at present living in two states with different social systems. . . . Nevertheless, attempts are being made to foster an awareness that German history has more to it than some theory of our simply being neighbours in the two successor states to the former German Reich. First of all, the special shared responsibility of the Germans in both German states for the legacy of their history has to be mentioned. One is particularly conscious of this 'community of responsibility' of the Germans on days which we keep to commemorate the National Socialist tyranny and some of its specific after-effects. So on the anniversary of the outbreak of war, 1 September, when we meet someone from Leipzig or Dresden we see them in a different way from someone from Warsaw or Cracow, because in 1939 the former stood, like us, on the side of the aggressor nation, while the latter belong among the victims. That is why it was a good thing, and showed convincingly an awareness of the reality of German history, when on the fortieth anniversary of the outbreak of war a joint call for peace was put together by the Protestant churches in both German states.[14]

In the context of the debate on stationing of American intermediate-range missiles on West German territory, and the counter-measures threatened by the Soviet Union (meanwhile some 90 SS–12/22 missiles out of a total of 700 Soviet medium- and short-range nuclear missiles were deployed in East Germany and Czechoslovakia), the concept of a 'community of responsibility' became a key phrase in statements by politicians in both German states, together with an expression used for the first time by Honecker in 1983, 'the coalition of reason'. When in October 1983 it became clear that the USSR was preparing to station additional short-range

14. R.v. Thadden, 'Thesen zum Geschichtsverständnis und seiner Rolle in den Gesellschaftsordnungen der Bundesrepublik Deutschland und der Deutschen Demokratischen Republik', in Deutscher Bundestag (eds.), *Deutsche Geschichte und politische Bildung. Öffentliche Anhörung des Ausschusses für innerdeutsche Beziehungen des Deutschen Bundestages*, Bonn, 1981, p. 19

missiles on East German territory, the official newspaper of the SED
published a letter to Erich Honecker from the Lutheran parish church
and graveyard supervisory board at Loschwitz, a part of Dresden:

> The idea fills us with horror, that the stationing of American nuclear
> missiles in Western Europe, which we all condemn, would be followed by
> reciprocal counter-measures on our territory and we and our children
> would have to live directly alongside nuclear missiles. We would like to
> offer you our support and at the same time to beg you most strongly to
> continue the dialogue between the two German states and to widen it, so
> that trust can grow as the basis for a partnership of peace and security: in
> your own words, 'a coalition of reason'.[15]

The printing of this letter by the newspaper was unusual in that the
East German régime had hitherto always taken care that the armaments of Warsaw Pact states were not criticised openly. The cooling
in the climate of world politics and the renewed arms race had led,
in the GDR also, to the emergence of a relatively independent peace
movement, though naturally not comparable to that in West Germany in terms of numbers. The SED's tactic was to react with
flexibility and tolerance towards gatherings of the 'spontaneous'
peace movement held alongside the government-sponsored 'official'
rallies, so long as they confined themselves to general demands for
stopping the arms race and for disarmament. In the context of the
situation at the end of 1983, a certain amount of anxiety about the
developing threat appears to have been generally shared, so that the
letter from the local church undoubtedly expressed the disquiet felt
also by the GDR leadership.

However, the East German régime's tolerance of the activities of
the independent peace movement during the period of greatest
controversy on the national security issue in the Federal Republic
should be seen also in the light of Eastern efforts to suggest to the
West Germans that they should have a permanent interest in
détente. An inquiry conducted in Bonn about rapprochement between the two Germanies since the invasion of Afghanistan came to
the following conclusions:

> A policy of détente between the two Germanies is in the national interest
> — on that much there is currently consensus among political leaders in
> the Federal Republic and the GDR. The future development of inner-
> German relations, however, is dependent upon various imponderable

15. *Neues Deutschland*, 22 October 1983

external factors. If the conflict between the USA and USSR should worsen, inner-German relations would not remain unaffected. . . .

The GDR wants above all, by behaving cooperatively towards the Federal Republic, to maintain the economic relations which are vital to it, and in this way to stabilise its own system. At the same time it would like to weaken the alliance between the FRG and the United States. The various activities under the peace heading also serve this purpose. The Federal Republic wishes by its policies to secure the free existence of Berlin, to reinforce economic, cultural and personal ties with the other half of Germany, and in this way to preserve national cohesion. To secure peace is the first priority of both German states.[16]

Among Soviet economists, in particular, the prevailing view seems to be that the measures for modernising the economy which Gorbachev announced in the spring of 1985 will continue to fail in their objective unless they are widened to include the Comecon countries, and that the price to be paid would be some limited recognition of the national interests of member states. It would also mean that for the time being the East German leadership would not, at Moscow's behest, raise any serious new obstacles in its relationship with the FRG. The landmark visit to West Germany in September 1987 by Erich Honecker laid a diplomatic foundation for what could become the most substantial improvement in Inner-German relations since Willy Brandt's *Ostpolitik* in the early 1970s. Nevertheless, in their policy towards the West, the SED leaders have continually to take account, not only of Soviet interests and sensibilities, but also of the lasting distrust of some of their own immediate neighbours. In a remarkable interview with the Paris newspaper *Le Monde*, the East German party chief and Head of State talked with unusual frankness on the subject:

We do not want our neighbours to be worried by the trauma of the two German states possibly joining together again. It should not be forgotten that the two countries have quite different social orders and belong to different alliances. . . . If one wants to speak of a 'common basis', then this is the interest which citizens of both the GDR and the FRG have in maintaining peace in Central Europe, and in a peaceful future for themselves and their children.[17]

16. S. Kupper, 'Festhalten an der Entspannung. Das Verhältnis der beiden deutschen Staaten nach Afghanistan', in *Deutschland Archiv*, 10, 1983, p. 1065
17. *Le Monde*, 8 June 1985

Occasional envious references in the Polish and Czechoslovak party press to the growing volume of trade between the two German states, or accusations of political blindness towards West German revisionism are expressions of continuing scepticism, given the fact that the SED from time to time still evokes the option of reunification. The purpose is to create doubts about East Berlin's political reliability. In the Soviet party press this undercurrent of suspicion was articulated very clearly in June 1985 in a leading article in *Pravda* by 'O. Vladimirov', to which special significance was attributed, because the author was then the First Deputy Head of the International Relations Section of the Soviet Communist Party Central Committee, Oleg Rachmanin:

> Departures from the Marxist-Leninist course are in one way or another linked with nationalistic tendencies. As regards internal policies, that means a watering down of Marxist-Leninist ideology, the emergence of modified theories of 'national communism' and intensified interest in the national question *per se*. At the level of relations with other socialist countries, the appearance of nationalistic tendencies is bound, without a doubt, to weaken international relations. Nationalism which takes the form of veiled, but at the same time barely concealed, hatred of Russia and anti-Sovietism, undermines the unity and resolution of the socialist peoples and damages socialism as a whole, as well as each individual country.[18]

With the resolution on *Deutschlandpolitik* adopted by the Bundestag on 9 February 1984, against the votes of the Green Party, the concept of a shared German 'community of responsibility for peace and security in Europe' entered into official policy in Bonn. A few months after the start of missile deployment and in a period of no dialogue between the superpowers (the Soviet Union had left the negotiating table in Geneva as a protest against NATO's weapons modernisation programme) this document, supported also by the SPD Opposition, signalled that polarisation between the main West German political camps was decreasing and that the Kohl/Genscher government was trying to maintain continuity in the *Deutschlandpolitik* of its predecessors, in substance as well as in style.

18. *Pravda*, 21 June 1985

Resolution of the German Federal Parliament on the State of the Nation in Divided Germany, 9 February 1984 (extract)

Relations between the two Germanies are influenced in very large measure by the relations between the two superpowers, the USA and the Soviet Union. The Federal Republic of Germany and the GDR share a community of responsibility for peace and security in Europe; both must try to achieve an easing of the international situation. War must never again start from German soil. The German Bundestag affirms that policies on Germany are at the same time policies for peace in Europe. Thus European peace policies are in our national interest. The Germans wish to live together in peace and to serve peace in Europe.

On the basis of their shared history, the Federal Republic and the GDR do indeed have a special obligation to ensure that no additional tensions arise on German soil which would lay an unnecessary burden on East–West relations. This 'community of responsibility' of the Germans in Europe nevertheless reaches its limits at the point where it touches on vital alliance interests or gives encouragement to the idea that the two German states could go their own way in defence policy. In an interview with German radio in the autumn of 1984, the President of the Federal Republic, Richard von Weizsäcker, preferred to speak of the Germans' 'responsibility for the climate' of the East–West relationship. This is how he used the expression:

> I believe there is no doubt whatsoever that, if we want to have a positive effect on the climate, we must address ourselves to the East–West relationship as a whole. The Harmel Report, the foundation for the Alliance policy of linking two goals inseparably together — on the one hand the capability and readiness for defence, and on the other the use of this defensive capability to achieve détente between East and West, but without setting limits on either side — these goals can only be achieved between East and West as a whole. It is unthinkable that a situation of détente could be introduced in central Europe if the temperature between East and West as a whole has dropped to freezing point. For this reason, it is also very greatly in the interests of relations between the Germans themselves that they do not make inappropriate attempts to pursue some special avenue of their own. So then, at bottom we always come back to recognising the same thing: We form part of this overall climatic situation ourselves.[19]

19. R.v. Weizsäcker, 'Probleme der Deutschland- und Europapolitik', interview on German external broadcasting service, *Deutschlandfunk*, 19 August 1984, in *Informationen. Bundesminister für innerdeutsche Beziehungen*, 17, 1984

Armed Forces 1982

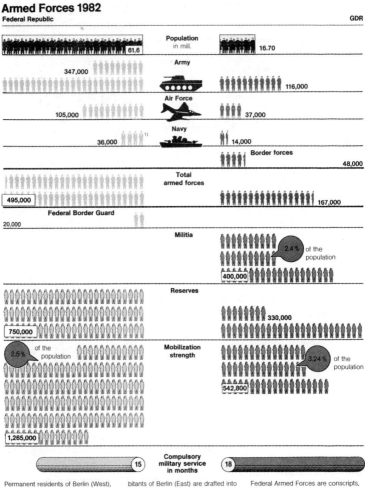

Federal Republic

GDR

	Population in mill.	
61.6		16.70

Army
347,000 | 116,000

Air Force
105,000 | 37,000

Navy
36,000 [1] | 14,000

Border forces
48,000

Total armed forces
495,000 | 167,000

Federal Border Guard
20,000

Militia
400,000 — 2.4% of the population

Reserves
750,000 | 330,000

Mobilization strength
1,265,000 — 2.5% of the population | 542,800 — 3.24% of the population

Compulsory military service in months
15 | 18

Permanent residents of Berlin (West), on account of the city's four-power status, are not called up for service in the Federal Armed Forces. They may serve voluntarily, however. By contrast, inha-

bitants of Berlin (East) are drafted into the GDR's armed forces, in contravention of the city's four-power status which applies to Berlin as a whole. 45.1 per cent of the personnel of the

Federal Armed Forces are conscripts, 12.7 per cent regulars, and 42.2 per cent temporary regulars.[2]

[1] Including 6,000 reserves on retraining each year
[2] Comparable statistics for the GDR are not known.

Source: Facts and Figures, p. 25

Comparison of strengths – NATO and Warsaw Pact 1983

A comparison of conventional ground forces embraces forces readily available in Europe, including North American reinforcements and all Warsaw

Pact troops west of the Urals. In the case of divisions, the equivalents have been stated which allow for the differences in manpower, weaponry and

technical equipment. As France and Spain do not participate in NATO's integrated structure they have been left out of consideration.

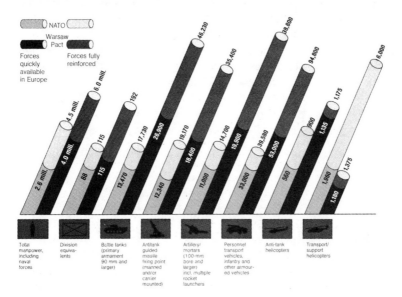

Total manpower, including naval forces — Division equivalents — Battle tanks (primary armament 90 mm and larger) — Antitank guided missile firing point (manned and/or carrier mounted) — Artillery/mortars (100-mm bore and larger) incl. multiple rocket launchers — Personnel transport vehicles, infantry and other armoured vehicles — Anti-tank helicopters — Transport/support helicopters

Source: Facts and Figures, p. 26

Position of the two German states in their military alliances (1982)

	NATO				Warsaw Pact	
Defence spending in bill. US dollars	308.4	196.3	24.6	10.2	257	300
Armed Forces in 1000	5,022	2,108	495	233	4,400	5,799
Gross national product in bill. US dollars	6,087	3,071.4	720.5	175.5	1,715	2,435
Gross national product per capita in US dollars (1981 prices)	9,783	12,482	11,032	9,914	5,991	6,040
National Budget in bill. US dollars	1,872.2	741	215.7	86.1	545.5	844.5
Population in mill.	568.9	232.1	61.6	16.7	270	380.4
Defence spending as % of gross national product	5.1	6.4	3.4	5.8	15.0	12.3
Defence spending as % of national budget	15.5	25.0	10.7	11.2	44.4	33.5
Defence spending per capita in US dollars						
Armed Forces per 1000 of the population						

Source: Facts and Figures, p. 27

4 / The Risks and Opportunities of a Central Position

No people in Europe in this century have so violated the laws of peace as have the Germans. Success and failure alike in German foreign policy since the war can be put down to one fact: that the two halves of Germany represent a nation in the heart of Europe whose actions or omissions have a direct bearing on the stability and peace of Europe.

Since its establishment in 1949, the Federal Republic of Germany has subordinated its foreign policy to the more general aim of stabilising peace and security in Europe, promoting arms control and contributing to the resolution of conflict. The early and fundamental decision on integration in the Western Alliance fixed irrevocably the guidelines of Bonn's international relations. The Federal Republic is a participant in East–West relations, being closely involved in the process of the formation of Western opinion, under the guiding influence of the USA. The FRG can lend its weight to the common defence effort, as well as in the strategic negotiating process. Through its readiness for dialogue with the East and its dependable and predictable policies it can help to create calm and aid the relaxation of tensions in Central Europe. However, because of its geographical position, history, and political allegiance, it cannot play the part of a European Third Force, nor seek a realignment of forces in Central Europe.

With the conflict between East and West, Germany not only lost her historic central position, but was actually relegated to the periphery, since the frontier between the two antagonistic power blocs exactly coincided with the line dividing the two Germanies. For the time being traditional German policies with a *Mitteleuropa* perspective could not, realistically, be reintroduced. Whereas Bismarck had to ask himself whether the European balance of power could bear the considerable weight of a united and powerful Germany, without causing her neighbours undue concern and thus bringing them together against the Reich, the peripheral position into which Germany has slipped since 1945 creates an entirely new situation. Today, to overcome the division of Germany would depend upon the division of Europe being removed first.

It follows naturally, therefore, that Bonn's foreign policy only began to rediscover its Central European perspective at the moment when détente reduced the confrontation between the power blocs and lowered the barriers to mutual contact. For Germany still lies at the heart of Europe and now, in the nuclear age, has to get on with its neighbours to the East and to the West even more than in Bismarck's time. Just as no country in its foreign relations can escape from the general conditions imposed by the international environment, neither can it for long evade the demands imposed by its geographical position.

The Continuity of Geography

The French historian Fernand Braudel, in his theory of overlapping layers of time, distinguishes between the short time span of historical events, the intermediate span covered by social and economic developments, and the long timescale of underlying factors or structures which hardly change. The most permanent of such structures he identifies as the continuity of geography, and he proposes relating the whole historical process to such layers of almost unchanging structures, in order to think it over afresh against this background. In his book devoted to Bismarck's Reich, the historian Michael Stürmer also refers back to the categories of structural history, in order to make clear the European background of Germany's national history. At the same time, however, he rightly warns against basing the interpretation of historical events too rigidly upon theories of continuity:

An absolutely unified theoretical construction cannot be at the same time the starting point of the performance and the end or fifth act of a drama which brought on such unavoidable catastrophes. The history of events seems to be warning us that history is made by people, that greatness, ambition, responsibility and guilt belong to its fabric, and that only a little of what happened had to happen in the way that it did. Structural history seems to insist that the movements of longer duration, the pattern of everyday life and the structures of politics, leave little room for action and decision, and that the idea of free will is nothing but an illusion. The latter theory is important for insight into the limitations on human action, the former for the lasting possibilities of human progress. What remains in between is left to the historians, albeit there are no solutions.[1]

According to this, the major structures can provide only the wider framework, within which certain developments are more likely than others. In spite of this reservation, one still cannot get away from the fact that, in the case of German history, there is a quite specific geographical continuity: her central position in Europe. This constant of German history is described by the historian Hagen Schulze in his history of the Weimar Republic:

> The major constant of German history is its centre position in Europe; Germany's fate lies in its geography. . . . These are the basic features of Prussia's existence: central position, insecure frontiers; fear of hostile coalitions and of war on two fronts; separation from East and West as well as arrangements with both, and an internal constitution reflecting external circumstances. In the course of time this all reappeared in changing forms, becoming all the more determinant, the greater the concentration of German power became.[2]

The American professor of politics David Calleo also tends towards a view of her central position as determining Germany's fate. In a study of the role of Germany in world history from Bismarck to the present day, he comes to the following conclusion:

> The German Problem does not somehow emanate from some special German 'character'. Imperial Germany was not uniquely aggressive, only uniquely inconvenient. Whatever faults and ambitions the Germans had were amply shared by the other major nations of the modern era. But unlike Britain, Russia, or the United States, the Germans lacked the space to work out their abundant vitality. Moreover, because of geography, Germany's vitality was an immediate threat to the rest of Europe. Modern Germany was born encircled. Under the circumstances, whatever the lesson of the wars between Germany and its neighbors, it cannot be found merely by analyzing the faults of the Germans.[3]

Germany's position in the middle of Europe was not just a burden for the Germans; it was a continual problem for Europe. It gave rise to pressures and counter-pressures, longings, threats, anxieties, conflicts, wars. But from it also came cultural interchange, diversity of thought, and the meeting of minds between Germans and their neighbours. Forty years after the end of the Second World War,

---

1. M. Stürmer, *Das ruhelose Reich. Deutschland 1866–1918*, Berlin, 1983, p. 12
2. H. Schulze, *Weimar. Deutschland 1917–1933*, Berlin, 1982, p. 18
3. D. Calleo, *The German Problem Reconsidered. Germany and the World Order. 1870 to the Present*, Cambridge, 1978, p. 206

Wolf Jobst Siedler, a Berlin writer and publisher, described the change which has taken place in Central Europe:

> Europe has gained one thing from the breakup of the former German Reich. For the first time in their history the Germans have turned themselves unreservedly towards the West; the power of the gigantic shadow which had fallen across Europe's centre was able to bring about what Western ideas could not achieve on their own. History itself had forced Germany to turn its face westwards and that is true for the people in the Eastern half of the country almost more than for those living under the protection of the Atlantic Alliance. It is this inner change of direction rather more than the outward weakening, which allows Europe to look kindly upon German affairs. . . .
>
> But when the West won Germany for itself, it gave up the rest of Europe in return. It won only half of Europe, and not only in the geographical sense. The two European empires lost in wars this century were really the Eastern part of the West, and the Western part of the East. What is Vienna without Lemberg and Trieste, or Berlin without a view towards Vilna and St Petersburg?[4]

Sixty years after Friedrich Naumann's plea for a structured *Mitteleuropa*, in which the two central powers, Germany and Austria, would be surrounded by their partners to the south and east, there is again much talk about the *Mitteleuropa* concept. Very varied motifs come together in this discussion, among them geography, culture and the needs and desires which cross all boundaries. The repellant effect which the Soviet system exerts on its western satellites, along with their own strong consciousness of their traditions and of differences in mentalities and lifestyles, lead to an urge for relaxation, for opening up, which many governments even in the Warsaw Pact countries do not reject out of hand. When Czechs, Poles and Hungarians talk of the special character of *Mitteleuropa*, they frequently mention the distance to the Soviet Far East, and emphasise what it is that the nearest parts of the Soviet empire have in common with Europe. When people in the Federal Republic consider *Mitteleuropa* there is, on the one hand, a reawakening of German cultural interest in Central and Eastern Europe, which is in no way a rejection of the fundamental worth of Western civilisation; on the other hand, a concept of *Mitteleuropa* which has been refined in political discussion embraces a certain distancing from the West and

4. W.J. Siedler, 'Was im Mai 1945 wirklich geschah. Längst bevor Europa seine Welt verspielte, verlor es seine Vernunft', in *Frankfurter Allgemeine Zeitung*, 4 May 1985

hence takes the *Ostpolitik* a stage further. The Swiss journalist François Bondy has taken a critical view of this:

> The ambiguity of the catchword '*Mitteleuropa*' lies in the fact that for some this *Mitteleuropa* is supposed to differentiate itself as far as possible from an 'Eastern bloc' as befits its cultural and political traditions — journals in France such as *L'Autre Europe, Alternative, La Lettre internationale,* are devoted to this theme — while on the other hand the new German yearning for *Mitteleuropa* means a distancing from the West, that is, its goal is diametrically opposed to the above. One could say it would be only natural for each part of Central Europe to want to distance itself from its 'protective power'. But this would be to forget the difference between a community imposed by force and an alliance freely entered into; the asymmetrical is represented as symmetrical, as if Western and Eastern Europe were both 'occupied' in similar fashion.[5]

Both Reich and nation-state came to an end in the defeat of 1945. A generation after 1945 the Germans are again beginning to ask about cause and direction in their history. The answers given in the immediate postwar period are no longer the only ones conceivable. Attempts to find a special path for Germany in Europe are stirring again. Questions about the German nation are linked with a new search for security in Central Europe. The diplomat Henri Froment-Meurice, formerly French Ambassador in Moscow and in Bonn, sees in this a challenge for French foreign policy:

> This is really no simple task. On the one hand we must try to shape matters in the West as irreversibly as we possibly can; on the other hand we have to fight against the finality of the situation in the East; to get more and more unity in the West, ever less separation from the East. Is this squaring the circle? That is, nevertheless, the double duty laid upon us. It arises of necessity from the existence of a Europe whose line of partition runs right through German territory. Germany is a house with two facades. The French have to get used to it and not worry themselves, if the Germans look ever more frequently through the windows facing east; but they must encourage them to use the western side even more often, by adding some large extra windows. Foreign policy is a form of architecture.[6]

5. F. Bondy, 'Selbstbesinnung. Selbstbestimmung: Kultur und Integration', in W. Weidenfeld (ed.), *Die Identität Europas*, Bonn, 1985, p. 76
6. H. Froment-Meurice, 'L'Allemagne entre l'Est et l'Ouest', in *Géopolitique*, 6, 1984, p. 78

Tradition in German Foreign Policy

A whole system of related terms, concepts and principles is employed in a country's portrayal to itself of its external relations. One
indispensable aid in this is reference to past experience and the
significance of earlier situations, for the traditions of a country's
foreign policy have a strong influence on the present as well. Yet
after 1945 the past seemed to have lost all significance for German
attitudes towards its future in Central Europe. History then meant
nothing more than memories of ruin, of tyranny and barbarity, the
collapse of Germany's empire and the loss of the nation-state.
Friedrich Meinecke, the elder statesman of German historiography,
wrote a book at that time which raised the question of whether
nearly every event in Germany's past had not been a step on the
road to 'the German catastrophe'.

The German Question has always been the question of where in
Europe the Germans belong: looking Westwards or wandering
between East and West; recognising their geographically central
position or breaking out of it? This was the vital question for
domestic as well as foreign policy in Bismarck's day. Despite the
discontinuities in German history in the last hundred years, the
same questions were and are continually posed anew and require
answers from responsible statesmen, always keeping in view the
continually changing patterns in international relations.

The answers found by German foreign policy makers from the
founding of the Reich in 1871 until Brandt's *Ostpolitik* a century later
lead the Berlin historian Arnulf Baring to distinguish three basic
patterns, three different attempts to find a solution:

(1) A kind of balance achieved through a complex set of relationships on all sides, represented by Bismarck, Stresemann and
Brandt;

(2) a break-out from the central position by grasping for hegemony over the territory of Europe and Western Asia, embod-
ied by Hitler;

(3) dissolution of the German nation state, for the good of the
Germans and the general good of Europe, in the supranational empire of medieval Christendom, uniting the traditions of Western, Southern, and Central Europe; to this
Adenauer felt he belonged.[7]

7. See A. Baring, 'Die Wurzeln der Bonner Ostpolitik', in *Europäische Rundschau*, 4,
   1974, pp. 59ff.

In view of the military confrontation of the superpowers in Central Europe, the powerlessness of a beaten and disarmed Germany and the practical impossibility of pursuing a third way between the blocs in the middle of international conflict, any revival after 1945 of Bismarck's idea of a balancing function for Germany was doomed to failure from the start. The choice of Western-style democracy became the basis of the Federal Republic's security and of its whole rationale as a state, both as regards internal and external policies. Only with the beginning of détente did the Germans win back part of their traditional freedom of action.

In 1971, Waldemar Besson, a professor of politics at the University of Constance, reached the following conclusions about the long-term effects of changing European and international circumstances upon the conflict between tradition and historic experience in German foreign policy:

> After twenty years history of the Federal Republic, we see that the Germans are unable to escape from their past in their role in Europe, and so today the fundamental question is posed as to how far the tradition of a primary option for the West, which Adenauer initiated, can be brought into harmony with the constant factors of the earlier experience? At all events it is evident that Bonn's foreign policy has lost the certainty of attitude and objectives which characterized the 1950s in the face of new challenges. A bridge needs to be built to join post-1945 Germany with the basic geographical and historical factors of the German situation, factors which the rigid dualism of two hostile blocs at the beginning of the 1950s seemed to have almost obliterated.
>
> It is therefore by no means argued that the Adenauer tradition is in the course of being replaced by another, as if the Germans could turn back the clock. Historical developments are not accomplished so simply. It is rather the case that a kind of synthesis of both traditions is in the making, Adenauer meeting Bismarck, and thus the experience of security meeting the desire for a more active shaping of national history.[8]

The setting aside of an active *Ostpolitik* during the Cold War was in one sense unavoidable, but in another sense temporary and provisional. That the Germans in their central position needed in the long term an understanding with the East as well as their ties with the West — this recognition is found as early as the mid-1950s in the

---

8. W. Besson, 'The Conflict of Traditions: the Historical Basis of West German Foreign Policy', in K. Kaiser and R. Morgan (eds.), *Britain and West Germany. Changing Societies and the Future of Foreign Policy*, London, 1971, p. 62

speeches of the first West German Chancellor. In many respects, the statement of policy which Konrad Adenauer made on 9 September 1955 on the occasion of his first (and only) visit to Moscow, already contains important elements of the détente concept of the 1970s:

> The highest good, which should be defended by every German, is peace. We know only too well how much was suffered, particularly by the Soviet and the German people, in the last war. . . . Finally, every person in Germany knows that our country's position would place us in special danger in the event of an armed conflict. . . .
>
> Whenever the conditions are fulfilled, under which a system of security can be built which will bridge the chasm between East and West — the Federal Republic will not withhold its cooperation. . . . In the shaping of our relations with the peoples of the Soviet Union, we wish [for ourselves]: peace, security, economic cooperation and the avoidance of tensions.[9]

Just fourteen years later, Chancellor Brandt, in his first statement of government policy, formulated the objectives of the 'new *Ostpolitik*' as follows:

> Our national interest does not allow us to come between West and East. Our country needs cooperation and agreement with the West and understanding with the East.
>
> But against this background I say most emphatically that the German people also need peace — peace in the full meaning of the word — with the peoples of the Soviet Union and with all the peoples of Eastern Europe.[10]

To be sure, the *Ostpolitik* of the 1970s also rested on the firm foundation of the Federal Republic's membership in the Western Alliance system. However, the treaties signed with the East freed Bonn from the self-restraint imposed upon it in the 1950s in its dealings with the countries of Eastern Europe. In the words of a Geneva-based specialist in East–West relations, Curt Gasteyger:

> In practice this meant, in line with the dual strategy of NATO, solidarity with the Alliance had to be the starting point for their opening towards

---

9. K. Adenauer, Declaration in Moscow on 9 September 1955, quoted in B. Meissner (ed.), *Moskau-Bonn. Die Beziehungen zwischen der Sowjetunion und der Bundesrepublik Deutschland 1955–1973. Dokumentation*, Cologne, 1975, pp. 85f.
10. W. Brandt, Government declaration of 28 October 1969, quoted in H. Haftendorn et al., *Die Aussenpolitik der Bundesrepublik Deutschland*, Berlin, 1982, p. 328

the East; indeed, it meant basing their security on unswerving allegiance to the former, while giving an extra political dimension to the latter, through a series of agreements on renunciation of force. The more intensive *Ostpolitik* conducted via numerous trips between Moscow and Warsaw, Prague and East Berlin, freed them from all kinds of political handicaps within the Western Alliance and from the stigma of 'aggressive revisionism' with which they were charged by the East. Bonn thereby proved that concern for military security could perfectly well be combined with a political settlement with likely opponents. It can also be argued against this, that with the exception of the Berlin Agreement, in which its interests were defended by the three Western powers, in none of the other treaties negotiated directly by Bonn did its membership in the Alliance bring it any more advantages than it had achieved already.[11]

The transition of the Federal Republic from collaborator to pace-setter for the efforts at détente in Europe was of course supported officially by its Western allies, but there were undercurrents of alarm among both Americans and French regarding the long-term effects of normalisation with the East. In a memorandum to the American President early in 1970, Henry Kissinger set out his thinking on a possible loosening of German ties with the West:

> The most worrisome aspects of *Ostpolitik*, however, are somewhat more long-range. As long as he is negotiating with the Eastern countries over the issues that are currently on the table — recognition of the GDR, the Oder–Neisse, various possible arrangements for Berlin — Brandt should not have any serious difficulty in maintaining his basic pro-Western policy. . . . But assuming Brandt achieves a degree of normalization, he or his successor may discover before long that the hoped-for benefits fail to develop. . . .
>
> Having already invested heavily in their Eastern policy, the Germans may at this point see themselves as facing agonizing choices. It should be remembered that in the 1950s, many Germans not only in the SPD under Schumacher but in conservative quarters traditionally fascinated with the East or enthralled by the vision of Germany as a 'bridge' between East and West, argued against Bonn's incorporation in Western institutions on the ground that it would forever seal Germany's division and preclude the restoration of an active German role in the East. This kind of debate about Germany's basic position could well recur in more divisive form, not only inflaming German domestic affairs but generating suspicions among Germany's Western associates as to its reliability as a partner.[12]

11. C. Gasteyger, *Die beiden deutschen Staaten in der Weltpolitik*, Munich, 1976, pp. 67f.
12. H. Kissinger, Memorandum to President Nixon, quoted in idem, *The White House Years*, London, 1979, p. 529

Among many French with an awareness of history, the conclusion of the German–Soviet Treaty in August 1970 awakened associations with 'Rapallo'. The name of this Northern Italian spa town, where in April 1922 the Russians and Germans suddenly and surprisingly reached an agreement, on the fringes of an economic conference in Genoa, has for over six decades been a symbol of the way in which German policies swing between East and West. It resurfaces whenever there is any move towards Moscow, actual or potential. Subconscious fears of this kind have affected a wide variety of observers, including André Fontaine, now Editor, but at that time head of *Le Monde*'s foreign desk, when he speculated in 1971 about the long-term effects of Brandt's *Ostpolitik*:

> If the close integration of Europe is not brought about first, it would be surprising if Germany, with its fantastic material wealth and economic power, does not return to the see-saw policies which have twice already led Europe to the brink of ruin. In the midst of the Cold War, Robert Schuman, whose perspective was a wide one and who knew what he was talking about, used repeatedly to argue, against those who spoke of 'containment' of the USSR, that Germany also had to be 'contained': that was the main reason for his commitment to European unity. One must make best use of the presence of men at the top in the Federal Republic whose love of peace and European convictions are beyond question, in order to work out with them structures which would bind Germany sufficiently tightly for one to be able to feel sure that its dynamism will in future be placed at the service of peace and the development of the continent, and never again be used in the attempt to dominate.[13]

Behind these reactions lies the central question of whether the Federal Republic with its *Ostpolitik* is regarded by its Western associates primarily as a partner sharing a common frame of reference, or if Bonn's contribution to détente should rather be interpreted as arising from circumstances which are specific to German history. This question did not require an unequivocal answer as long as Germany's Eastern policies were in step with those of the West in general. Only with the increasing erosion of détente in the late 1970s and the open crisis at the beginning of the 1980s did argument about where the Germans stood break out once more.

13. A. Fontaine, 'Paris–Bonn–Moscou. L'autre triangle', in *Le Monde*, 11 September 1971

Commitment to the West and to Western Values

The irritations over the Germans which have arisen in recent times, particularly in other Western countries, have led to doubts about German loyalty to the Alliance. They result, in the first instance, from the tensions inherent in the Germans' geographical situation and the threats coming from outside it. With détente and the attempts to ease inner-German relations, there was once again a heightened awareness of the fact that the divisions of Europe, of Germany, and of the city of Berlin had not been wiped away, and that the Federal Republic is for this reason forced to pursue 'Western policies' under the peculiar conditions of a partitioned Germany. The question to be asked today is whether the unprecedented commitment to the West which originated with Konrad Adenauer, and which cut right across the centuries-old tradition of Germany's central position, will continue in the future to determine the guiding principles of the Federal Republic.

The first Chancellor was resolute in his decision to integrate the FRG into the West, since for him a lasting democracy in Germany would not be founded without its complete integration in the Western community of nations. This decision was understood by him as an historic rejection of all idea of a 'separate path for Germany' and of the restless switching to and fro between East and West. Adenauer formulated this principle of West Germany's basic position in his first government statement of 20 September 1949:

> But there is no other way for the German people to follow, to bring them back to freedom and equality of status, after the total collapse resulting from National Socialism, but the way of ensuring we walk back up again together with the Allies. . . . We should have no doubts that, by our origins and basic attitudes, we belong to the world of Western Europe. . . .
> All our work will be carried out in the spirit of Western Christian civilisation and with respect for justice and human worth.
> We hope — this is our goal — that with God's help we will succeed in leading the German people forward, to make their contribution to peace in Europe and in the world.[14]

Even in Adenauer's own party, the choice of a Western course and founding of a Western-style state were not without opposition. Jakob

---

14. K. Adenauer, First Government Declaration on 20 September 1949, quoted in Auswärtiges Amt(ed.), *Die Auswärtige Politik der Bundesrepublik Deutschland*, Cologne, 1972, pp. 153f.

Kaiser, until 1948 CDU Chairman in the Soviet zone of occupation, tried in the early postwar years consciously to take up the classical concept of *Mitteleuropa*, and advocated an independent path for Germany as middle-man and 'bridge' between East and West. In a New Year's article, on 1 January 1947, he wrote that Germany had a 'function as the nation in the middle':

> If we want the recovery of Germany, we can only act on the basis that Germany is placed in between East and West. This situation, fateful in its consequences, yet full of opportunities, does not lead to an 'either/or' choice between Western or Eastern blocs, but to the 'not only/but also' of understanding and accommodation between peoples, to recovery starting in our own hearts and minds.[15]

The decision for a Western state, taken without Jakob Kaiser's support but with that of the Social Democrats led by Schumacher, paved the way for a new foreign policy orientation. Friends and foes of the new state were clearly defined. The principles guiding the Federal Republic began to be revealed as differing from the principles followed by Bismarck's Reich. In the words of Alfred Grosser:

> At the same time it strengthened its internal cohesion through a double refusal, through an ideology based on a double negative: rejection both of the Nazi past and of the Communist present. . . . By good fortune, the Federal Republic saw itself as forced permanently to take a stand *against* something, so that this double negative in some measure formed the basis for the legitimacy of a state whose sovereignty was poorly secured, a state which united only part of the nation. . . .
>
> The overwhelming majority of Germans have, since 1947–8, without being fully aware of it, made a choice which really is an exception in the twentieth century. They have preferred the justifiable defence of political values, associated by them with the values of economic life, to the unity of the nation: rather no reunification than any form of reunification which would bring with it even the least danger of Communist influence in a reunited Germany.[16]

Can the Germans manage this state of affairs in the long term? There are some indications that the consensus which existed at the

15. J. Kaiser, 'Deutscher Weg 1947', in *Neue Zeit*, 1 January 1947, quoted in H.-P. Schwarz, *Vom Reich zur Bundesrepublik. Deutschland im Widerstreit der aussenpolitischen Konzeptionen in den Jahren der Besatzungsherrschaft 1945–1949*, Stuttgart, 1980, 2nd edn, p. 311
16. A. Grosser, *Geschichte Deutschlands seit 1945. Eine Bilanz*, Munich, 1977, 4th edn, pp. 126ff.

founding of the Federal Republic is breaking down, and that a reawakened awareness of the special nature of the centre position again brings with it a distancing from the West and a rejection of the conditions imposed on Germany's existence by European integration. Recently, after many West Germans said 'No' to NATO's arms modernisation, the idea of a third way between East and West again met with approval, and fringe political groups now propagate the idea of releasing the FRG from the Atlantic Alliance and the ties with Western Europe. With a critique of European culture and civilisation clearly formulated in terms of national identity, efforts are once again in hand to find a specifically German standpoint, as so often in the past, by deliberately setting aside values and principles which are characteristic of the Western nations. Something of this was conveyed by the electoral programme of the Berlin Alternative List parties in January 1985:

> If Federal German state power today maintains once again the strongest armed forces in Western Europe, that is for us no cause for newly-awakened pride or national feeling, no contribution to the defence of values and freedoms, but a reason for us to demand a fundamental change in West German foreign and defence policies. . . .
>
> We want to use the legal, economic and political anachronism of Berlin's situation as an opportunity for Europe-orientated policies with the long-term aim of freeing both German States from military pacts, as offering real peace for Europe. . . .
>
> NATO and the Western allies will be requested to reduce their military presence in the Federal Republic and West Berlin and eventually to end it. . . .
>
> It cannot be excluded that the developments we demand could lead to the military superiority of the Soviet Union in Europe. We are however convinced that the danger of war which arises from existing security policies is far more likely to lead to an actual outbreak of war.[17]

Günter Gaus, in an attempt in 1983 to 'fix the location' of the Germans, outlined various possibilities of the two German states getting together as a result of what, in his opinion, is an increased threat of war in Europe:

> Where Germany lies, its exact location, would be easy to find in the event of another war in Europe: in the middle of where the killing starts, whether the war is waged with nuclear or conventional weapons. . . .
>
> If there was a nuclear-free zone in Central Europe, where Germany

17. *Wahlprogramm der Alternativen Liste*, Berlin, 1985, pp. 315ff.

lies, safeguarded by a balance of forces in Europe, and guaranteed by
Washington and Moscow, could attempts not be made to form confeder-
ations in some parts of the region?

Virtually everything stands in the way of such pan-European cooperation. The uncertainties will grow. West Germany lacks its own sense of
balance, because it has for so long depended on the balance of foreign
forces; intolerance, in some cases already fixed in legal form, resignation
and irrationality will be rife. I am worried that Germany's misfortunes
have not yet reached their lowest depth.[18]

The idea that only freedom from military alliance, or at least some
distancing from both superpowers, would offer prospects for Germany's future, in many respects ties in with the ideas and concepts
of the early postwar years. At the same time, the international
background to Germany's situation in the 1980s is so fundamentally
different from that of the immediate postwar years, that a decoupling from the alliance systems in East and West would disturb the
already precarious equilibrium of the postwar world in the whole of
Europe, whose fate it is not up to the Germans to decide on their
own.

In response to these isolated attempts to find answers to the
German question, Chancellor Kohl once more referred to the political standpoint of the Bonn Government in his report on the state of
the nation in divided Germany, dated 27 February 1985:

> Thirty years ago the Federal Republic of Germany acquired sovereignty
> in international law, while at the same time continuing to pursue the aim
> set out in the thinking behind the Locarno Treaty: the integration of
> Germany in a Europe of free peoples. . . . Our commitment to Europe is
> an historic decision, a political fact, and above all a decision for the
> European values of Christianity and of the Enlightenment, of social
> justice and the rule of law.
>
> We stand both internally and in our external relations, on the side of
> freedom. The common values of the western community of nations and
> our democratic political order are in harmony with each other. For us
> there is no middle way between democracy and dictatorship. Anyone
> seeking a third way puts our liberty at risk.
>
> Konrad Adenauer's unequivocal choice of a Western commitment, of
> values shared with the free democracies, was a rejection of all attempts to
> find a separate national path. This fundamental choice is and remains
> irreversible.[19]

18. G. Gaus, *Wo Deutschland liegt. Eine Ortsbestimmung*, Hamburg, 1983, pp. 276ff.
19. H. Kohl, 'Bericht zur Lage der Nation im geteilten Deutschland', 27 February
    1985, in *Bulletin. Presse- und Informationsamt der Bundesregierung*, 24, 1985, pp. 198f.

The Third Way in Political Literature

The idea of a 'third way' between East and West has always exerted a particular fascination in Germany precisely because of her central geographical position. This is especially true of early postwar political writing, and also that of the 1980s, when the escape from conditions imposed by the international situation is associated with the dream of another model of society.

Hans Werner Richter and Alfred Andersch, editors of the journal *Der Ruf*, called for a democratic form of socialism which would constructively combine both individual freedom and state planning. They conceive of Germany as the testing ground of two ideological areas, where two social orders are in the melting-pot:

> Germany lies in the centre between East and West and has to live with both. By taking up the socialist ideology of the East and the democratic ideology of the West, it can unite both in itself on a higher plane. In this union it will be able to find in the future that form of state which corresponds to its own being and development.[20]

In contrast to *Der Ruf*'s ideas, the neutralism which Ulrich Noack, the Würzburg historian, advanced in the late 1940s had nothing to do with socialist views. According to Noack's ideas, Bismarck provided a model with his idea of the 'honest broker': in his view, Germany ought not to shut herself off but, on the contrary, should be open on all sides and present herself as a middle-man between East and West. In his view only the transformation of Germany into a demilitarised neutral zone could reduce international confrontation and ensure peace. The idea of a 'two-way economic integration' of Germany and its surroundings fits into this view:

> This could come about through the sharing of increased production and exports between East and West. This would allow the aid continually given by the West to be reimbursed in a planned way, without Germany appearing as a troublesome competitor in Western markets. Yet at the same time, with the approval of treaty and alliance partners and without disadvantage to the West, Germany can set to work, processing Russian raw material surpluses for Russia. In this way, the tensions between the worlds of East and West, arising from economic and social differences,

20. H.W. Richter, 'Deutschland — Brücke zwischen Ost und West', in *Der Ruf*, 4,1 October 1946, quoted in H. Schwab-Fehlisch (ed.), *Der Ruf. Eine deutsche Nach-kriegszeitschrift*, Munich, 1962, p. 49

would finally be dissolved through the well-planned working of a world determined on peace.[21]

Pragmatic economic ideas meet together in Noack's thought with more or less fanciful flights of the imagination. Thus he believed that a 'tough mental attitude' would be sufficient to combat the danger that the power-vacuum created through a neutralised Germany could allow the Soviet Union to make further advances.

In contrast to this concept of a third way for a future Germany of pacifist hue, Wolf Schenke, with his group *Dritte Front* (Third Front), calls for a neutral but strong united Germany, which would function as the focal point for a self-sufficient and independent Europe, equidistant from both superpowers. In the 1950 manifesto of the group he writes: 'The values which we again have in mind and to which we must give reality, are European, growing out of Greece and Rome, blended with Christianity and Teutonic traditions, brought to full bloom in Italy, France and Germany. Americanism is no less foreign to these values than Russian Bolshevism'.[22]

Most of the alternative concepts from the postwar period underestimate the consequences of the political and ideological antagonism between East and West, in view of which Konrad Adenauer pursued his policy of Western integration with the support of a large majority, especially after the SPD Opposition's change of course on foreign policy in 1960. The student protest movement in the late 1960s and the peace movement from the end of the 1970s began to question this approach. With the worsening of East–West relations after the invasion of Afghanistan, German intellectuals began raising the question of whether the all-too-close relationship between the Bonn Government and the American superpower was really reconcilable with 'special German interests', and they linked with this the theme of questioning the value of the Alliance. German writers from both East and West expressed their worries about peace at joint meetings. Through these it became clear that the idea of a special mission for Germany was again playing its part.

The disquiet over dependence on the superpowers was most clearly articulated by the writer Günter Grass, who then lived in

21. U. Noack, 'Aufruf zur Rettung des Friedens durch Neutralisierung Deutschlands', 4 December 1948, quoted in Schwarz, *Vom Reich zur Bundesrepublik*
22. W. Schenke, 'Aufruf zur Gründung der Dritten Front', 1 October 1950, quoted in R. Dohse, *Der Dritte Weg. Neutralitätsbestrebungen in Westdeutschland zwischen 1945 und 1955*, Hamburg, 1974, p. 85

Berlin; at the second Berlin Writers' Conference in April 1983, he
called for 'the right to resist':

> I am suffering from the current state of our major ally. I feel bitter that
> the present government of the United States of America is incapable of
> democratic impulses any more, but is rather more set on violence and the
> use of its strength. . . . There would be no acquittal of the West's guilt, if
> it continued to trust in this leadership, with its threats of genocide. But it
> is not just up to Western governments to question critically the USA's
> claim to leadership, as long as these governments — the West Germans
> above all — have neither the power nor the will for West European
> autonomy. Rather, everyone who, in simple terms, values his own life and
> that of his enemy too, should ask himself whether he wants to offer any
> resistance.
>
> Because I belong to the West and speak out for the Western idea of
> democratic freedom, I see it as my duty to resist. But before all else, it is
> the German experience, including the missed opportunity in 1933 to
> resist at the first signs of genocide which requires me to make this
> decision. . . . If we succeed, in the course of the second Berlin Conference,
> in overcoming the present feeling of powerlessness, then we writers ought
> to regard ourselves as part of the peace movement in East and West and
> should speak out for the right to resist.[23]

A critical distancing from the Western superpower is also detectable
in Peter Bender's brilliant appeal for a 'European Europe', which
gives a new dimension to the idea of a third way:

> After 1945, the USA was the ideal, in which strength, goodness and
> beauty seemed in a wonderful way to combine; with Vietnam they
> became wicked imperialists, and now it is time for them by degrees to
> appear as normal human beings. That would provide the best basis for us
> to get closer together again. Western Europe can hardly wish to be allied
> with Superman, a normal major power is difficult enough as an ally. . . .
>
> As a democratic superpower, America considers it natural for all the
> democracies to gather together in mutual agreement around the USA,
> this forming the model for all decision-making. The Western Europeans
> have recognised, by a large majority [81 per cent of West Germans at the
> beginning of 1980], that they must remain allied to the United States, but
> that they should stand politically in between Washington and Moscow.
> To the Americans, every move away from America appears to be a

23. G. Grass, Speech made to the 2nd Writers' Conference, 22–23 April 1983, in
    Zweite Berliner Begegnung. Den Frieden erklären, Darmstadt/Neuwied, 1983, p. 49
24. P. Bender, *Das Ende des ideologischen Zeitalters. Die Europäisierung Europas*, Berlin,
    1981, pp. 204f.

rapprochement with the Soviet Union; in Western Europe it is a return to normality for those who are as keen Europeans as they are democrats.[24]

Shortly before the elections to the Bundestag in the spring of 1983, the American Enterprise Institute brought together a representative cross-section of German views on the theme of the foreign policy options of the Federal Republic in East–West relations. In a critical appreciation, the London-based historian Roger Morgan came to the conclusion that the search for orientation was a natural consequence of the uncertainties of the international scene at the beginning of the 1980s, but that Bonn's fundamental commitment to the West in its foreign policy is not in doubt:

> Those who shaped the early foreign policy of the Federal Republic, and the citizens of the country as a whole, drew their sense of security from a certain set of ideas received during the cold war years: the Soviet Union was the enemy, the United States and the Western allies were friends, and German security demanded a total commitment to the West. During the years of détente (whether preached by de Gaulle, Nixon, or Brandt), the Germans accommodated themselves to another set of beliefs: their security depended partly on the military strength of the West, to be sure, but it also depended on 'joining the crowd' of Western nations determined to create links of interdependence and cooperation with the Soviet bloc. Now, in the post-détente era, neither of these sets of orthodox beliefs is sufficient. It is no wonder that the Germans show signs of confusion: few of them are prepared to follow President Reagan back to the certainties of the cold war years, and even fewer of them will follow the leaders of the 'Green Alternative List' in the easy assumption that détente is still a developing reality.[25]

25. R. Morgan, 'The Debate over German Security Issues: a Synopsis', in *Germany: Keystone to European Security. A Symposium — AEI Foreign Policy and Defense Review*, 3–4, 1983, pp. 66f.

5/The Nation-state and German National Consciousness

In Europe's more recent history, the German Question has invariably assumed a dual character. While continuing to question the existence of Germany as a state, it also covers the problem of the development of democracy in Germany and of how deep-rooted it is. In Europe's historical experience, the combination of a unified German state with a non-democratic ruler has twice threatened the existence of neighbouring countries and other powers associated with Europe.

With the cessation of hostilities and occupation of Germany in 1945 came an end to the period in which Germans could choose for themselves the framework of their life as a single entity. The question of Germany's existence as a state was for the time being so decided that the country was partitioned. The German collapse meant at the same time also an end to two centuries of policies intended to maintain the balance of power in Europe. Now arguments over the reestablishment of a power balance in the second half of the twentieth century are carried on by the two new world powers — the USA and the Soviet Union — in the middle of Europe. The partitioning of what was once the most powerful central-European nation had an additional consequence, however, in that each German state sees itself as the representative of one of the opposing systems. The question of democracy in Germany has been resolved in such a way that a bourgeois-liberal democracy in the West confronts a counter-model with Communist characteristics in the East.

At the same time the East–West conflict is for the Germans not simply a question of foreign and security policy or of belonging to different alliance systems. East Germany has become, after its superpower leader, the country which sets economic standards on its side, and both, thanks to their geographical and strategic position, carry great military weight. Beyond this, each German state claims that since its foundation, partly in response to the internal and social changes in the other part-state, it has been able to make binding the commitment to the basic values of its own social order. However different, even diametrically opposed, the motivations and goals of the two Germanies, their policies are in all respects intended to be taken as a model within each competing system.

How the Two German States understand their Nationhood

In the Federal Republic, all politically important decision-makers support the declared intention of preserving national unity. Whereas the GDR tried, at the beginning of the 1970s, to push the countries' division to the point of national separation, and accordingly gave constitutional expression to this, the Federal Republic's attitude to the nationality question has shown a continuity unbroken to the present day.

In the Basic Law, the entire German people is still required 'to achieve by free self-determination the unity and freedom of Germany'. In the Letters on German Unity at the conclusion of the Moscow Treaty and the Basic Treaty with the GDR, the Bonn Government stated that the Treaties '[do] not conflict with the political objective of the Federal Republic of Germany to work for a state of peace in Europe in which the German nation will recover its unity in free self-determination'. The decisions of 31 July 1973 by the Federal Constitutional Court on the Basic Treaty establish the constitutional legal framework for the 'German nation' and 'the people of the German state', alongside the framework in international law provided by continuing Four Power responsibility for the whole of Germany; taken together, this precludes the recognition of the GDR by the FRG in international law at any time in the future.

The Basic Law of the Federal Republic of Germany, 23 May 1949 (Preamble)

The German People . . . conscious of their responsibility before God and men,
    animated by the resolve to preserve their national and political unity and to serve the peace of the world as an equal partner in a united Europe,
    desiring to give a new order to political life for a transitional period,
    have enacted, by virtue of their constituent power, this Basic Law of the Federal Republic of Germany.
    They have also acted on behalf of those Germans to whom participation was denied.

The entire German people are called on to achieve in free self-determination the unity and freedom of Germany.

Letters on German Unity, 12 August 1970 and 21 December 1972 (extract)

In connection with today's signature of the Treaty . . . the Government of the Federal Republic of Germany has the honour to state that this Treaty does not conflict with the political objective of the Federal Republic of Germany to work for a state of peace in Europe in which the German nation will recover its unity in free self-determination.

Decision of the Federal Constitutional Court on the Basic Treaty, 31 July 1973 (extract)

The clear position in law of every government of the Federal Republic of Germany is: We must base our position upon the existence of Germany as a whole as set out in the Basic Law, in which it is 'anchored', with an [all-] German nation, and an [all-] German governmental authority. When reference is made to a 'German nation', as embracing the whole of Germany, no objection is raised to this if it is at the same time understood as a synonym for 'the people of the German state'.

With the dropping of the Federal Republic's claim to sole representation of the German people, at the end of the 1960s, and the new political maxim of 'two states in one Germany', the SPD–FDP coalition began to differentiate between 'state' and 'nation'. By way of compensation for legalising the status quo of partition, the idea of the 'nation' now took on the function of representing 'the bond holding divided Germany together'. From the existence of one nation was derived the right to pursue self-determination for all Germans as a policy objective. Emphasis was shifted from the reestablishment of political unity to the maintenance of the sense of belonging together of people in both countries, through an intensification of inner-German relations.

This new emphasis in the way the nation was to be understood was intended to overcome the classic contradiction between the nation as a cultural entity and the nation as 'people of a state', as defined by the German historian Friedrich Meinecke in his study *Weltbürgertum und Nationalstaat* (*World Citizenship and the Nation-state*,

1907), through use of the concept of 'a nation rooted in the consciousness of the people'. In the early postwar years the Social
Democrat, Carlo Schmid, a skilled lawyer, had introduced this
'nation-rootedness' in the justification of claims based upon nationality, in order to compensate in some way for the shortcomings of the
actual situation regarding the unity of the German people. On 8
May 1949, in the Parliamentary Council, fourteen days before the
Basic Law was finally passed, he described his goal as being the
unity of Germany in freedom:

> The Germans do not bring this yearning for unity up out of some
> romantic subconscious — a dangerous thing, which can so easily lead
> people astray. No, they get this will for unity from something very
> elementary. The roots of this desire lie in the consciousness that what
> belongs together must come together, if there is to be any true order in the
> relationships between peoples. . . .
>
> But such a union would take no account of history if it did not create
> the preconditions for German unity in freedom, in the freedom of the
> whole and of the individual. This union must have as an object the
> creation of similar conditions of democratic life everywhere in Germany,
> West and East.[1]

In the context of the first report by the SPD–FDP coalition on *The
State of the Nation*, in January 1970, Chancellor Brandt defined the
concept of the nation with reference to its roots in the consciousness
of the people as an expression of an enduring sense of a common
bond among the people of one nation:

> Twenty-five years after the unconditional surrender of Hitler's Reich the
> concept of the nation forms the bond holding divided Germany together.
> In the concept of the nation, historical reality and political will unite.
> 'Nation' embraces a wider significance than common language and
> culture, state or social order. The nation is based on the enduring sense of
> a common bond among the people of a nation. No one can deny that in
> this sense there exists and will exist a German nation for the foreseeable
> future. Furthermore: one could say that even the GDR acknowledges
> itself a part of this German nation in its constitution.
>
> We must, in my opinion, have a historical and political perspective if
> we speak of the state of the nation, or if we back up the demands for self-
> determination of the German people. History has divided Germany
> because it is guilty, or at any rate not without guilt on its part; history will

---

1. C. Schmid, Speech to the Parliamentary Council, 8 May 1949, quoted in C.C.
   Schweitzer (ed.), *Die deutsche Nation. Aussagen von Bismarck bis Honecker. Dokumentation*, Cologne, 1979, 2nd edn, pp. 317f.

decide when and how these demands can be met. So long as the Germans can find the political will not to give up these demands, hope will remain that future generations will live in a Germany whose political order the Germans as a whole can work out together.[2]

More than fourteen years later, the Christian Democrat Chancellor Helmut Kohl referred in similar terms to the continued existence of a sense of unity and insisted on the need to find a free and democratic answer to the national question:

> Our most important legal and moral position remains the claim of all Germans to freedom and self-determination. The unity of the nation must and shall be fulfilled first and foremost in the freedom of its people. . . .
>
> Marked by many centuries of shared historical experience in the heart of Europe, we Germans see our nation's unity as wholly self-evident.
>
> The historic and political changes which have taken place on German soil have not erased the consciousness of national unity.[3]

Since the creation of the Federal Republic, all governments in Bonn have shown continuity in the pursuit of the goal of Germany unity and have tried to uphold and promote the feeling of solidarity among the German people in both states as indispensable to this. In the GDR, in contrast, the national concept and national question have undergone various changes, reflected, among other things, in the re-draftings of their constitution since the founding of the state.

The wording in the first constitution of 1949, on the way they understood themselves and the German nation, was based not only on a claim to be the sole representatives of the German nation — a claim also contained in the Basic Law of the Federal Republic — but was couched *expressis verbis* in all-German terminology. First the preamble refers to 'the German People' as having given itself this constitution, then Article 1 states unequivocally that Germany is 'an indivisible democratic republic'. However, in the second constitution of 1968 two contradictory lines may be discerned: a recognition of German unity is contained both in the preamble, which speaks of 'the entire German nation', and in Article 1, according to which the GDR is 'a socialist state of the German nation'. But against this there is set the establishment and further development

---

2. W. Brandt, 'Bericht zur Lage der Nation', 14 January 1970, quoted in H.E. Jahn, *Die deutsche Frage von 1945 bis heute. Der Weg der Parteien und Regierungen*, Mainz, 1985, p. 459
3. H. Kohl, 'Bericht zur Lage der Nation im geteilten Deutschland', 15 March 1984, in *Bulletin. Presse- und Informationsamt der Bundesregierung*, 30, 1984, p. 262

of the socialist system of society and the upholding of 'the principles of socialist internationalism' (Article 6). Finally, the changes in the 1974 constitution took account of the East German leadership's need for a stricter separation from the FRG, by deleting all references to Germany as a whole, while at the same time stressing the importance of the ties with the USSR and the community of socialist states. According to the new preamble, the people of the GDR has achieved 'its right to socio-economic, political and national self-determination'.

Constitutions of the German Democratic Republic (extracts)

Constitution of 7 October 1949

Preamble: The German People, imbued with the desire to safeguard human liberty and rights . . . and to promote a secure peace . . . have adopted this Constitution.

Art. 1(1): Germany is an indivisible democratic republic, the foundations of which are the German Länder.

(2): The [German Democratic] Republic decides on all issues which are essential to the existence and development of the German people as a whole. . . .

Constitution of 9 April 1968

Preamble: Borne by the responsibility of showing the entire German nation the road to a future of peace and socialism, . . the people of the German Democratic Republic have given themselves this socialist Constitution.

Art. 1: The German Democratic Republic is a socialist state of the German nation. . . .

Amendment of 7 October 1974

Preamble: In continuation of the revolutionary traditions of the German working class and in consequence of the liberation from fascism, the people of the German Democratic Republic has, in accord with the processes of historical development in our time, realized its right to socio-economic, political and national self-determination and is building an advanced socialist society.

Art. 1: The German Democratic Republic is a socialist state of workers and farmers. . . .

It is precisely the insistence of the Federal Republic on the continued existence of the nation's unity that has been perceived by the
GDR, since the beginning of the 1970s, as a hindrance to its full
recognition as the second state on German soil. The Brandt-Scheel
government's offer to East Berlin in its *Deutschlandpolitik* and *Ostpolitik* to strengthen intra-German cooperation, was considered there as
a threat to the formation of independent East German national
consciousness. Whereas the attitude of the SED régime towards the
national question was marked, until the end of the 1960s, by the
desire in principle for the reunification of Germany and by their
holding on to the assumption of an all-German nation, the slogan of
the GDR's altered *Deutschlandpolitik* was to be 'demarcation'. Thus,
in a speech made in 1971 on the eve of the twenty-fifth anniversary
of the founding of the Socialist Unity Party, the then party chief and
Chairman of the Council of State, Walter Ulbricht, declared categ-
orically:

> The *bourgeois German nation*, which developed in the process of the transi-
> tion from feudalism to capitalism and which existed in the framework of a
> unified state from 1871 to 1945, *exists no longer*. The GDR is the socialist
> German nation-state, in which the formation of a socialist nation is in
> process of completion. That is why already certain irreversible facts have
> come into being.[4]

Under the leadership of Erich Honecker, who replaced Ulbricht on
3 May 1971, the distancing from the concept of one nation, endorsed
by the 8th Party Conference of the SED (June 1971) was further
reinforced. In his report to that party conference from the Central
Committee of the SED, Honecker argued vehemently against the
view put forward by the Bonn Government that there existed *one*
German nation and insisted that, on the contrary, a process of
demarcation between the FRG and GDR was being carried out. At
the time of the constitutional changes in the autumn of 1974, which
were intended to bring the wording of the 1968 constitution into line
with the reality of the ideological interpretation, Honecker stated:

> Since our liberation from fascism by the glorious Soviet Union, our
> people have continued the revolutionary traditions of the German work-
> ing class and carried them to victory in giving reality to their right to
> socio-economic, political and national self-determination. . . .

4. W. Ulbricht, 'Rede zur Vorbereitung des 25. Jahrestages der SED, 13 January
   1971' in *Neues Deutschland*, 14 January 1971

The German Democratic Republic of today is an internationally recognised, sovereign socialist state, which has linked its present and future indissolubly and forever with the land of Lenin and the other countries of the socialist community. . . . In this connection, it is advisable to define the character of our state and to make clear, in Article 1, that the German Democratic Republic is a socialist state of workers and farmers.[5]

However, this position was neither supported by the East German population, nor found credible in Eastern Europe as a whole. By December 1974 the SED leadership had given way on a small point, in that it distinguished between 'citizenship of the GDR' and 'German nationality'. Basically, this brought them back to the definition in the Ulbricht constitution of 1968. Finally, in the early 1980s, Erich Honecker unexpectedly declared his renewed support for a future Communist unification of the two Germanies. On 15 February 1981, at a district delegate conference of the SED on future prospects of the national question, he said:

If today certain people in the West talk big about Greater Germany, and behave as if the reunification of the two German states lay closer to their hearts than their wallets do, what we would like to say to them is: Be careful! One day Socialism will knock on your door too [loud applause], and if the day comes when the working people of the Federal Republic start on the socialist reshaping of the Federal Republic of Germany, then the question of reunification of both German states would look entirely different. [Loud applause] There would be no doubt at all about what our answer would be then.[6]

In parallel with the reappearance of this perspective, there was an extension of the GDR's claims regarding its history. No longer were simply the traditions of humanism, revolutionary forces and the movement of the working class claimed as the historic foundations of the GDR, but — as repeatedly stated in official statements — the whole of German history without limitations of time, space or 'class determination'.

Since the early 1980s the GDR leadership has deliberately stressed a return to German and to Prussian traditions. In accordance with this, Frederick the Great (whose statue again stands on the Unter den Linden in East Berlin), Martin Luther and, most

---

5. E. Honecker, 'Rede in der Volkskammer, 27 September 1974', quoted in Schweitzer, *Die deutsche Nation*, pp. 611f.
6. E. Honecker, 'Rede auf einer SED-Bezirksdelegiertenkonferenz in Berlin', 15 February 1981, in *Neues Deutschland*, 16 February 1981

recently, Bismarck (despite continued criticism on certain aspects), have been honoured as great historic figures. By this means the GDR seeks to show itself as the defender of the best traditions of the whole German people, and the option of a 'Socialist Germany' as being kept open.

How 'Open' is the German Question?

'Denk ich an Deutschland in der Nacht, dann bin ich um den Schlaf gebracht.' ('If I think of Germany in the night, I can't fall asleep'.) This was once the judgement, in rhyme, of the poet Heinrich Heine. Nearly a century and a half later the contemplation of Germany in West and East gives rise to many sleepless nights, as latent fears of the European status quo being disturbed yet again by the Germans has become a recurring theme in international discussion. An extreme example of this is an article by the well-known American columnist William Safire, writing in the *New York Times* of 13 August 1984, under the eye-catching headline: 'Revanche is sweet'. Safire warns of the possibility of secret negotiations on reunification:

> German nationalism seems to mean more to Mr. Honecker than continued subservience to Moscow and more to Mr. Kohl than this generation's method of defending Western Europe. A decade from now, we will learn of the secret negotiations that took place in these years between Germans who put Fatherland ahead of ideology. It should not be a surprise; it's only natural. Would a reunited, neutralist Germany be a useful buffer between superpowers — or a way for the Russians to get the Americans out of Europe? Would it revive the nationalist spirit that led to two world wars?[7]

One month later, some remarks on the German problem made by the Italian Foreign Minister, the Christian Democrat Giulio Andreotti, attracted considerable attention and led to a good deal of diplomatic activity between Bonn and Rome. During a platform discussion at the national festival of *Unità*, the newspaper of the Italian Communist Party, he said the following, with reference to the postponement of Honecker's visit to West Germany:

> There are deep fears in many countries, starting with the Poles, and in other countries of the Warsaw Pact, but also in countries outside the

7. W. Safire, 'Revanche is sweet', in *New York Times*, 13 August 1984

Warsaw Pact. The fears are two-fold: we are all agreed that the two
Germanies maintain good relations with each other. This is a contribution to peace which no one under-estimates. But it should be made clear
that one ought not to go too far down that road; that is, one has to
recognise that pan-Germanism is something which must be overcome.
There are two German states and two German states they should
remain.[8]

Quite a different view was expressed by Edmund Osmańczyk, the
Polish writer and member of the Polish Parliament in Warsaw, the
Sejm, in a speech made to the Silesian Institute in Opole:

> Our neighbours on the other side of the Oder and Elbe are coming or
> have already come to terms with the frontier on the Oder and Neisse. But
> they will not come to terms with the division of Germany. Over the last
> hundred years, the modern German nation has been shaped for a long-
> term future. We are gradually learning to understand that the differing
> systems in the GDR and FRG do not affect national unity. The return to
> Prussian civic virtues in both German states has strengthened the oneness
> of the German nation more than it has impaired life under two different
> economic systems. . . .
> Neither of the two superpowers is going to let itself in for a united
> Germany based on a unified social order, since that would destabilise
> nuclear peace. On the other hand a confederation with two social orders
> would be a new model in a world divided by different orders of society, yet
> on the human plane absolutely one. The Germans could play a significant
> role for peace in the middle of Europe in this way.[9]

Discussion abroad was in part a reaction to the public efforts by
Bonn and East Berlin not to place unnecessary burdens on the
relationship between the two Germanies, in spite of the stationing of
missiles. Yet here too is reflected the traditional ambivalence of the
rest of the world towards the Germans. In 1983, shortly before his
death, the Italian writer and journalist Luigi Barzini published an
essay about the Europeans, in which he makes the future of our
continent dependent on Germany's decisions:

> Without Germany, the uniting of Europe would be impossible and
> meaningless, but if Europe were united with Germany included, all
> members would have to take on the German Question together. . . .

8. G. Andreotti, Platform discussion on the theme: 'Italian foreign policy and the
   development of democracy', 13 September 1984, in *La Republica*, 16–17 September 1984
9. E. Osmańczyk, 'Keine Angst vor deutscher Einheit', in *Die Zeit*, 10 August 1984

The future lies in the lap of the gods. It will probably once again be determined by Germany's decisions. And Germany is, as it ever was, a changeable, protean, unpredictable country, dangerous above all when it is unhappy.[10]

It would certainly be short-sighted simply to dismiss such utterances as the neurotic suspicions of neighbouring countries. In a very subtle analysis of the new attention being paid to the national question in the Federal Republic, the Cologne-based journalist Hermann Rudolph reaches the following assessment:

Among the surprising developments of recent years is a change in the way the German question is being discussed. While hitherto it often enough aroused suspicion, partly as representing an ever-renewed battle against resignation, partly as an obligatory exercise, now all at once it has become a highly explosive topic. . . .

This is happening, too, in a more open atmosphere than before. Points of view which hitherto were regarded as so obvious that they hardly entered into discussion, now appear all of a sudden to be worth questioning, in the literal sense. The position of the Federal Republic in the East–West conflict and in the Alliance is no longer taken as beyond doubt; rather, it has become the subject of new reflection and speculation. The same goes for the belief that German unity cannot be an operative goal of the Federal Republic's policies, at least not for the foreseeable future. The thought of policy being directed primarily in the national interest has become a great deal more attractive.[11]

At a historical symposium on 'Germany and the West', held at the end of 1983, the Cologne University historian Andreas Hillgruber distinguished between four strands of a 'diffuse revival of national-German tendencies':

1. A view of the GDR principally, but not solely, advanced by the DKP [West German Communist Party], which sees the GDR as a key 'socialist' country which, given favourable international conditions and the collapse of European equilibrium, would 'win over' a new German national state based on Marxist–Leninist 'socialism'.

2. A concept put forward by a 'Left' nationalist movement (aimed at bringing down the system in both East and West), of a more or less revolutionary German policy, attacking the dominant roles of the USA

10. L. Barzini, *Auf die Deutschen kommt es an. Die unzuverlässigen Europäer*, Hamburg, 1983, pp. 316f.
11. H. Rudolph, 'Die deutsche Frage — neu gestellt?', in *Mut zur Einheit. Festschrift für Johann Baptist Gradl*, Cologne, 1984, pp. 147f.

and the Soviet Union alike.

3. Ideas of the radical Right and [old] German nationalism, dreaming of the re-establishment in power-political terms of a fully sovereign German nation state as a major power.

4. What one might call 'a reformed national-liberal' concept of Germany, along the lines originally supported by the Federal Republic in its understanding of itself, actively promoted by the USA, and which great efforts were made to revive in the 1970s. Champions of this view do not regard the 'German Question' as 'finally' settled, precisely because they know that the continuation or re-establishment of a fully sovereign nation state, able to pursue its 'own way' in terms of power politics (comparable to Bismarck's Reich) is just not possible. They know moreover, the close interdependence between national self-determination and the future shape of Europe (i.e. with respect also for the view of 'balance' which has always been basic to the European order) as already outlined by the Founding Fathers in the preamble to the Basic Law. . . .[12]

In later remarks, Hillgruber warned insistently against 'upsetting' the relative strengths of these separate viewpoints. The unmistakable attraction exerted by the first three 'movements' relative to Germany's future was, in his view, directly linked to the fact that the West, in the first place the USA, had for over twenty years developed no new initiative on the German Question.

The view of the present Bonn Government has been given by Alois Mertes, Minister of State at the West German Foreign Office, in an article written shortly before his death:

The question is: do the Western powers really identify with our basic national concerns as set out in the Basic Law and the Germany Treaty, or do they merely pay them lip-service? During my years living abroad in Western countries I have often discussed this with Americans, British and French. The answer, I have to say, is: neither more nor less than they identify with the Poles' desire for freedom. There is in the West no specific identification with the desire for freedom of the Germans in the GDR. There is an identification with some interests, at any rate with the basic moral demands for individual human rights and national self-determination, of all the peoples who after 1945 fell under Soviet power. It is important in the present threatening situation, with weapons more dangerous than ever before in history, that first of all we, as representatives of Germany, are clear that even among those Americans, British and

12. A. Hillgruber, 'Westorientierung — Neutralitätsüberlegungen — Gesamtdeutsches Bewusstsein', in H. Köhler (ed.), *Deutschland und der Westen*, Papers of the Symposium in Honour of Gordon A. Craig, organised by the Freie Universität Berlin, 1–3 December 1983, Berlin, 1984, pp. 166f.

French who regard us the most benevolently, there exists no stronger identification with the Germans' desire for freedom than there is with that of the Czechs, Slovaks or Poles. That, actually, is the European dimension of the German Question. But I say that also in the sense that obviously no one can openly express support for the freedom of Poles, Czechs and Slovaks, and at the same time say that the Germans ought to stay divided. For the essence of Germany's division is not so much a question of frontiers, but rather of individual human rights and of national self-determination.[13]

A similar viewpoint has also been put forward, in Paris, by the expert on Germany, Joseph Rovan, when he takes the following position on the question of the relations between the Germans and their neighbours in the 1980s:

Germans, French, Poles and all other European nations must examine their national consciousness on the basis of its content. They cannot nowadays come to terms with Herder's historical nation, any more than they can with a Marxist or Darwinian concept of the nation. Therefore, the national reunification of the two German states cannot be an acceptable goal for the Germans in either the GDR or the FRG, and still less so for their neighbours, if it is, so to speak, 'blown up' to be the highest value attainable. The nation nowadays only has sense or value as a living framework for the values of liberty and human rights, as the historical site of various cultural developments and as providing the way towards the abolition of differences in the equality of individuals, of humanity. . . .

The right to self-determination for all peoples and nations in Europe, rather than the reshaping of states, could be the common objective of all Europeans.[14]

The Germans and their Fatherland

The more than 18 million people affected by the creation of the GDR on 7 October 1949 did not want to be either a second German state or to have a socialist order of society. In return for the German attack on the Soviet Union, they were put through a 'revolution from above', brought into the country with the Red Army. The years which followed saw a continuation of what began as this army marched in: in a massive migration, about 3 million Germans fled

13. A. Mertes, 'Westliche und östliche Interessen in der Deutschlandfrage', in *Politik und Kultur*, 3, 1985, pp. 8f.
14. J. Rovan, 'Verändertes Nationalbewusstsein? Ein Beitrag zur Entspezifizierung der deutschen Frage', in *Deutschland Archiv*, 10, 1984, p. 1039

from East to West between the end of the war and 13 August 1961. Partition really began only in the second decade of the GDR's existence, with the building of the Wall around West Berlin; yet even after 1961 the stream of refugees did not completely dry up.

The agreements signed in the 1970s undoubtedly helped to make the consequences of partition more bearable for people, yet this benefited least Germans in the GDR itself. For them — apart from pensioners and exceptions made for pressing family reasons — the prohibition on travel to the West still applied. From West to East, however, efforts to maintain contacts and family ties remained very intensive.

Some seven to eight million citizens of the Federal Republic visit the GDR every year, 20 to 25 million telephone calls are made annually from West to East alone. Through radio and television, the everyday realities of life in the West are continually present in the GDR; 80 per cent of all GDR citizens can receive West German television programmes. For their part, the East German media have only a limited impact in the West; they can be received, but have little effect on public opinion.

Despite the Eastern treaties, despite the hugely increased stream of visits and travel which followed and despite considerably greater efforts by the West German media to obtain factual information about the GDR, the question of how far these developments ensure the continuance of an all-German national consciousness is debatable. At the beginning of the 1970s the West German social scientist, Gebhard Schweigler, in his doctoral thesis at Harvard, presented a wide-ranging assessment of public opinion polls on this question; he summarised the results of these as follows:

> The division of the German Reich into Eastern and Western zones posed the German Question; the development of the German Democratic Republic and the Federal Republic of Germany into independent nation-states seems for the time being to provide the historical answer to this question. There can hardly still be doubts about that, despite many contradictions in official pronouncements and media views in both German states. Taken as a whole, the documentary material presented here allows no other conclusion to be reached. . . .
>
> The international recognition of the GDR . . . will strengthen national consciousness in the GDR and the FRG alike; that is, both countries will be separated further from each other in regard to their national consciousness, whereas they ought slowly to get closer together on the human plane. This means, however, that neither the status of the FRG nor that of the GDR will continue to be questioned.[15]

Travel in 1000

From the Federal Republic (incl. Berlin [West]) to the GDR[1]

Between 1961 and 1966[2] some 2-2.5 million people travelled from the Federal Republic to the GDR each year, whilst the number from Berlin (West) – from 1963 to 1966[3] – was between 0.8 and 2.5 million.

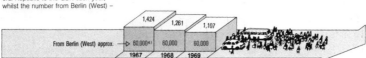

From the GDR to the Federal Republic[5]

Overall intra-German travel

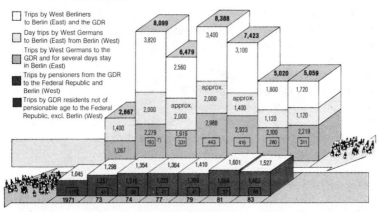

No exact figures are availabel for travel from the Federal Republic to the GDR up to 1961. Only since the erection of the Berlin wall and the increasing fortification of the intra-German border has it been possible to keep a more accurate count of trips from the Federal Republic to the GDR or Berlin (East). Conversely, there are no exact statistics for travel from the GDR to the West prior to 1953, primarily on account of the permeability of the intra-German border in the early fifties and the completely unhampered traffic in the whole of Berlin.

[1] From 1967 excl. approx. 1.4 million day trips annually by residents of the Federal Republic to Berlin (East) via Berlin (West). [2] Incl. the 1.4 million day trips mentioned under footnote 1. [3] Trips by residents of Berlin (West) to Berlin (East) on the basis of the pass agreements of 1963–1966. [4] Trips by residents of Berlin (West) to Berlin (East) with the permission of the pass office to attend to urgent family business, as from October 1966. [5] Up to 1961, excl. travellers to Berlin (West). [6] As from 1964, almost exclusively travellers of pensionable age, also a small number of functionaries, businessmen, lorry drivers, etc. [7] Incl. border-zone traffic (from July 1973). [8] November/December 1972.

Source: Facts and Figures, p. 99

Intra-German postal traffic

Telephone telecommunications between the two states in Germany were extremely difficult in the fifties and sixties. As all calls had to be hand-operated and there were few switchboards, long waiting periods were the rule. Not until the mid-seventies were the first STD lines introduced between the Federal Republic and the GDR. Their number has been increased since the agreement on postal traffic. Prior to 1970 there were no telephone communications at all between Berlin (West) and the GDR and Berlin (East). The number of telephone calls made to the Federal Republic and Berlin (West) cannot be registered.

Number of lines in both directions

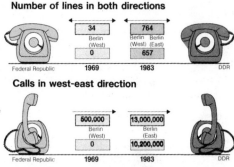

	34		764	
	Berlin (West)		Berlin (West) Berlin (East)	
	0		657	
Federal Republic	**1969**		**1983**	DDR

Calls in west-east direction

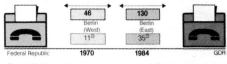

	500,000		13,000,000	
	Berlin (West)		Berlin (East)	
	0		10,200,000	
Federal Republic	**1969**		**1983**	DDR

Until the late sixties there were very few telegram and telex links between the two German states, with the result that telegrams took a long time to arrive. Telex lines existed only between a few official departments for the notification of disasters or traffic accidents. Since 1970 the number of links has increased steadily in both directions.

Telegram links in both directions[1]

TELEGRAMM	28		88	TELEGRAMM
	Berlin (West)		Berlin (East)	
	4[2]		21[1]	
Federal Republic	**1970**		**1980**	GDR

Telex links in both directions

	46		130	
	Berlin (West)		Berlin (East)	
	11[2]		35[2]	
Federal Republic	**1970**		**1984**	GDR

[1] Since 1971 fully automatic.   [2] Incl. those from Berlin (West).

Letters and parcels in millions

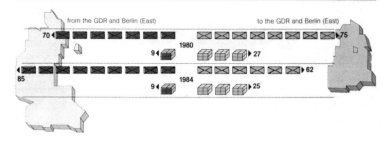

Ten years later, Karl Moersch, who had been Parliamentary Under-Secretary and Minister of State in the Bonn Foreign Office under both the Brandt-Scheel and the Schmidt-Genscher governments, interpreted the basic political realities of both German states in a similar way, describing them as 'definitive'. This was how he saw the situation, against the background of the historical development of German national feeling and the recurrent separation between German state and nation:

> German national history has always been full of contradictions. The equation 'state = nation' has never worked out smoothly. There always remained something left over which was hard to define. Should one not recognise that it does violence to the Germans and their history, if words are applied to them which originate somewhere else and which have a meaning which is clearly grasped there, but not by the Germans?
>
> One could perhaps get out of this difficulty by means of some sort of working concept, such as the 'extended nation' — but extended in a quite different way from that recommended for years by those in power in the GDR. What I mean is the term 'cultural entity'. No one can seriously dispute that the Germans in the Federal Republic and the Germans in the GDR could allow themselves to be brought together at least verbally under this heading.[16]

If one looks at the age structure of the German population in the mid-1980s, one sees that today only 30 per cent of all citizens in the two countries are fifty years old and over; only they have links through memory with the long-gone reality of a unitary German state. In five years it will be three-quarters of all Germans, in ten years over 80 per cent who will have grown up in a divided Germany. Now, the feeling of belonging does not depend on direct experience. It can also be instilled through history, tradition, the family; people can long for, hope for and dream of something they do not know. The results of more recent surveys allow conclusions to be drawn about national consciousness in the Federal Republic — the East Germans' usual policy on research and publishing is an almost total embargo on the details of such an explosive subject. Results in the FRG show a curious ambivalence, with more gradations than the shifts in generation would lead one to suppose. A Cologne-based sociologist, Erwin K. Scheuch, has found a very striking analogy for this phenomenon:

---

15. G. Schweigler, *Nationalbewusstsein in der BRD und der DDR*, Dusseldorf, 1973, pp. 196ff.
16. K. Moersch, *Sind wir denn eine Nation? Die Deutschen und ihr Vaterland*, Stuttgart, 1982, p. 108

The theme of national consciousness as a problem of the Federal Republic has similarities with the Loch Ness Monster. First similarity: it always appears different, depending on which side one sees it from, while the outlines remain indistinct. Secondly, national consciousness, supposedly our problem, is a media event — also similar to the creature in Loch Ness. And thirdly: when one finally gets it properly in one's sights, the object vanishes in the mist.[17]

Collected data show that the Germans, above all the younger generations, have difficulties with the words 'nation', 'state' and 'people', but only when limitations are placed on the area they are applied to. Identification with the Federal Republic as 'society', 'homeland' and 'state' certainly lacks the exclusivity that such an identification should have according to classical ideas of the nation-state. Several identifications are given at the same time, with the emphasis varying according to the area of association. Those questioned are capable of seeing themselves simultaneously as Germans and as citizens of the Federal Republic. At the same time they also identify themselves with Europe, and their understanding of 'German' also includes the abiding desire for reunification. These different kinds of idea generally exist quite unconnectedly in juxtaposition to each other, allowing no clear conclusions to be drawn regarding a more- or less-strongly formed consciousness of all-German nationality.

A similar ambivalence also characterises findings on the wish for and likelihood of reunification. Sample opinion surveys carried out by the Emnid Institute showed in 1953, the year of the second election to the Bundestag, a proportion of 18 per cent of the population in the FRG who regarded reunification as sure to happen. By the end of the 1950s this proportion had dropped to 5 per cent, and since the mid-1970s it has stood at about 2 per cent. The proportion of those who consider reunification unlikely rose between 1973 and 1983 from 53 to 60 per cent.

The development of expectations about a reunified state also makes its mark on the consciousness of common nationality. Whereas in 1974 70 per cent of those questioned still expressed the opinion that the FRG and GDR represented 'one German nation', and 29 per cent held the opposite view, by 1984 this had changed to 42 per cent and 53 per cent respectively, with the drop in feelings of national solidarity spreading beyond the teenaged and young adults.

17. E.K. Scheuch, 'Die deutsche Nation im Bewusstsein der Bevölkerung der Bundesrepublik Deutschland', in K. Weigelt (ed.), *Heimat und Nation. Zur Geschichte und Identität der Deutschen*, Mainz, 1984, p. 161

Question: Do you expect the division between the GDR and the Federal Republic to end in the foreseeable future, and that there will again be one Germany? (response in %)

	1951	52	53	54	55	56	57	58	59	73	83
Yes, definitely	10	6	18	13	9	10	10	4	5	2	2
Yes, perhaps	17	15	25	24	18	22	21	14	16	7	5
Don't know	36	41	36	43	43	43	39	46	51	32	33
No	28	28	16	16	27	22	27	34	24	53	60
No answer	9	10	5	4	3	3	3	2	4	6	—

Source: Emnid

Question: Would you say that the GDR and the Federal Republic represent one German nation or would you say that the two states do not belong to one German nation? (response in %)

	Total	Age groups				
		16–19	20–29	30–49	50–64	65+
1974						
One nation	70	64	65	68	74	77
Not one nation	29	36	34	31	25	22
No answer	1	1	1	1	1	1
1984						
One nation	42	26	34	39	50	60
Not one nation	53	71	61	56	42	37
No answer	5	3	5	4	8	3

Source: Emnid

Contrasting oddly with strong doubts about the chances of reunification actually coming about is the desire for reunification of a majority of nearly 80 per cent, a figure which for 30 years has hardly decreased.

Question: Are you personally for reunification of the two German states, against reunification, or are you indifferent to whether it takes place or not? (response in %)

	Sept. 1979	Nov. 1980	Jan. 1984
For reunification	79.3	76.9	79.6
Against reunification	3.9	7.0	3.9

Indifferent	16.2	15.2	16.2

Source: Forschungsgruppe Wahlen, Mannheim, Politbarometer survey for ZDF Television

On the supplementary question of whether European, i.e. West European, integration was more important and desirable than the reunification of Germany, preference was given to the European Community by a majority of respondents. But expectations directed towards the West have since been shaken. In 1983 19 per cent of all those questioned thought it certain or probable that in the year 2000 there would be a united Europe, whereas ten years earlier 47 per cent chose 'certain' or 'probable' as answers.

Question: Which do you consider the more urgent, the unification of the GDR with the Federal Republic, or a unified Europe? (response in %)

	1983	1973	1965
Unification of GDR and FRG	36	23	69
European unification	60	65	24
No answer	3	12	7

Source: Emnid

The rejection of reunification under an East German style of political and social system remains both clear and stable — even in the younger age groups. It may be that the correspondingly strong Western preference expressed by this is linked with the decreasing consciousness of 'one Germany'. Yet the proportion of those who support a neutral united Germany as the best solution of the German Problem is increasing:

Question: There are various different opinions on what a reunified Germany should look like. We have listed some possibilities here and would like to know which you would most prefer. (response in %)

	Total	CDU/CSU	SPD	FPD	Greens	Rest
Sept. 1979						
Like FRG	62.8	77.0	57.3	51.1	—	51.5
Neutral	31.1	20.6	40.8	46.0	—	41.3
Like GDR	1.7	2.2	1.4	0.3	—	2.2

Question: *continued*

	Total	CDU/CSU	SPD	FPD	Greens	Rest
Jan. 1984						
Like FRG	61.7	71.3	59.9	64.4	19.8	54.2
Neutral	36.6	28.5	38.4	35.6	79.3	38.7
Like GDR	1.3	0.2	1.5	0.0	9.9	4.7

Source: Forschungsgruppe Wahlen, Mannheim, Politbarometer survey for ZDF Television

Germany? Now, Where is That?

Anyone setting out today in search of the German identity will, as ever, come up against the problem of who and what is being referred to. Is it the Germans in the Federal Republic, or those in the GDR, or both? To see the problem in terms of language is not a suitable frame of reference either, since in other countries, too, German is spoken and German culture is alive. If one follows political and legal definitions, it must be accepted that, until the conclusion of a peace treaty, Germany continues within her frontiers of December 1937. The constitutional duty laid down in the preamble to the Basic Law 'to preserve its national and political unity' is also closely connected with the task of integration, 'to serve the peace of the world as an equal partner in a united Europe'.

Even forty years after the end of the war there is no simple, universally-accepted answer to this question, only the reality of complex identities and competing historical and political influences. At an earlier time, when arguments over the ideas of nationhood spread by the French Revolution were beginning to shape German national consciousness, Schiller complained:

> Deutschland? Aber wo liegt es?
> Ich weiss das Land nicht zu finden.
> Wo das gelehrte beginnt, hört das politische auf.

(Germany? Now where is that? I know not how to find this country. Where what is taught begins, political reality ends.)

From the same work, *Xenien*, comes also some famous verses by Goethe and Schiller on the German national character, about the transcending of the national by the personal, and which make clear that already in the past, German self-fulfilment revolved around

The German Reich on 31.12.1937

Source: Facts and Figures, p. 4

ideas of the individual and of the basic human need of Germans to live together.

> Zur Nation euch zu bilden, ihr hoffet es, Deutsche, vergebens;
> Bildet, ihr könnt es, dafür freier zu Menschen euch aus![18]
> (Germans, you hope in vain to build yourselves into a nation;
> What you can do is to make yourselves freer as human beings!)

It would perhaps be true to say that it is precisely because an identity based on nationality is unattainable that the possibility exists today of defining 'being German' otherwise than through differentiation from others. For just as an identity crisis in one's personal life is less likely to be overcome by changing outward circumstances than by coming to terms with one's inner self, so the

18. J.W.v. Goethe and F. Schiller, *Xenien*

politico-legal clarification of Germany's borders would hardly suffice to stop all questioning of the substance of Germany's identity as a society. In his speech to the 1985 Protestant Church Conference in Düsseldorf, Richard von Weizsäcker gave his view of the situation:

> What does it actually mean, 'German'? We are people like anyone else. Like others, we love our homeland. Certainly, our geographical position, our history, our many neighbours, and not least we ourselves, have cast both bright light and deep shadows.
>
> Time and again these things have brought about change. They have often made it difficult for us to understand our neighbours and ourselves. They have generally conferred on us no stability, and seldom a unity of existence; they have burdened us with separation. We are always having to learn afresh how to put up with these things, without becoming indifferent. We must and we can use them and bring good out of them, not only for ourselves, but for many other people too. . . . It is up to us to give the word 'German' a content with which we ourselves and the rest of the world will be able to live happily and at peace.[19]

At an early stage, an example was set by Germans who had been expelled from their homelands and by later refugees. Despite their bitter experiences — more than two million of those fleeing or expelled met their deaths — five years after the war they solemnly committed themselves to the renunciation of force and called for reconciliation and cooperation with the countries of Eastern Europe. On 5 August 1950, the association of Germans born in the former Eastern provinces announced the 'Charter of Germans expelled from their Homelands', in which they defined as follows their rights and obligations in postwar Europe:

> 1. We, the expellees, renounce vengeance and retaliation. For us, this is a solemn and sacred resolve in memory of the endless suffering which has been brought to mankind especially in the last decade.
>
> 2. We will support with all our power every initiative directed towards the creation of a united Europe, in which its peoples can live without fear or compulsion.
>
> 3. We will through hard and unremitting labour play our part in rebuilding Germany and Europe.
>
> We have lost our homeland. Displaced persons are strangers on this earth. God placed people in their own lands. To separate people by force from the land of their birth is to kill them in spirit.

19. R.v. Weizsäcker, 'Die Deutschen und ihre Identität', in *Deutscher Evangelischer Kirchentag Düsseldorf 1985. Dokumente*, Stuttgart, 1985, pp. 369f.

We have suffered such a fate and survived it. Therefore we feel
ourselves called upon to demand that the right to one's homeland be
recognised and acted upon as a God-given basic right of humanity.[20]

The integration of over 12 million German expellees and refugees is
without doubt among the greatest achievements of German postwar
history. It was and remains a service rendered by the Federal
Republic of Germany, on whose territory the overwhelming majority of expellees found a new homeland, that it has not allowed this
problem to become an explosive social issue in its own country or to
become a burden for Europe. The frontiers of the *Kleindeutschen*
nation-state created by Bismarck have, in the bare seventy years of
its existence, permanently shaped ideas of the political order to be
striven for in the area of Central Europe settled by the Germans, as
it has the consciousness of their nationhood. This is still true, even
when this nation-state has long been broken up as a result of Nazi
arrogance. But the memory of the *Kleindeutschen* state, in which the
Germans for the first time experienced their nation as a political
reality, has faded with the passing of the generations. What could
perhaps take the place of the national consciousness of 'little Germany' is today still unclear, or at any rate visible only in vague
outline. The following examples from the literature of the period
after the building of the Berlin Wall reflect this perplexity.

Der Vogel Schmerz	*The Bird of Pain*
Nun bin ich dreissig Jahre alt	Now I am thirty years of age
und kenne Deutschland nicht:	and I don't know Germany:
die grenzaxt fällt in Deutschlands	the frontier axe hacks through
wald.	Germany's wood.
O land, das auseinanderbricht	O land that breaks apart in
im menschen . . .	people . . .
und alle brücken treiben pfeileros	bridges go across but none have
	pillars.
Gedicht, steig auf, flieg himmelwärts:	Poem, rise up, fly heavenwards!
Steig auf, gedicht, und sei	Rise up, poem, and be
der vogel Schmerz.	the bird of Pain.

Reiner Kunze, *Der vogel Schmerz* (1963)

---

20. 'Charta der deutschen Heimatvertriebenen', 5 August 1950, quoted in *Erkläru-
    ngen zur Deutschlandpolitik. Eine Dokumentation von Stellungnahmen. Reden und Entschlies-
    sungen des Bundes der Vertriebenen — Vereinigte Landsmannschaften und Landesverbände*, pt. I,
    1949–1972, Bonn, 1984, pp. 17f.

Germany is not a model, it is a marginal and special case. Our political circumstances are not central, but eccentric. The Wall not only divides Germans from Germans, it divides us all from all other people. It blocks our thinking and our powers of imagination. It barricades not just one city, but our future. It illustrates nothing so much as ourselves: that which we still have in common. The only thing which we do still share together is our division. Our identity is that of being torn apart. Disunity, that is our identity.

Hans Magnus Enzensberger, Büchner Prize Speech (1963)

Politically divided for the foreseeable future, yet one in culture and history: having to live with this tension, like the curiously grown-together leaves of the *ginkgo biloba* (maidenhair tree), described by Goethe in a famous poem from his *West-östlicher Diwan* — this is what makes it especially difficult nowadays to be a German.

Ginkgo Biloba	*The Maidenhair Tree*
Dieses Baums Blatt, der von Osten	The leaf of this tree from the East
Meinem Garten anvertraut,	Entrusted to my garden here
Gibt geheimen Sinn zu kosten,	Has hidden meaning to be sampled
Wie's den Wissenden erbaut.	Such as would instruct the wise.
Ist es *ein* lebendig Wesen,	Is it but *one* living being
Das sich in sich selbst getrennt?	Which divides itself in two?
Sind es zwei, die sich erlesen,	Or two which then select each other
Dass man sie als *eines* kennt?	That they may be known as *one*?
Solche Frage zu erwidern	In reply to such a question
Fand ich wohl den rechten Sinn;	I surely found the answer true:
Fühlst du nicht an meinen Liedern,	Do you not sense in my poems
Dass ich eins und doppelt bin?	That I'm one, but also two?

J.W. von Goethe, West–östlicher Diwan (1819)

As an existential challenge, this conflict is also a constantly recurring theme in present-day literature, which reveals the reality of this continuing perplexity throughout the decades of partition. In a document approved in October 1947 by the First German Writers' Congress, authors from East and West formulated their concerns as follows:

For the first time since the barbarity in Germany was overcome, writers from all parts of the country have met freely together in Berlin. These are writers who, either in their homeland or as emigrés, have preserved the values of German literature. They see in our language and culture the guarantee of the inalienable unity of our people and land and the unbreakable link crossing all zonal frontiers, all party differences. . . .

We see forces at work which seek to banish the word 'German' from geography and history, and it would be foolish to the point of temerity if we were to turn a deaf ear to this danger. Bearing in mind the evil which the Nazi regime brought upon the world, it is our wish to make our contribution to reconciliation between East and West. What we do know is that we would inevitably sink into the complete loss of our culture, if there were no longer any consciousness of a single, living Germany.[21]

Thirty years later and in a completely altered international context, the West German writer Martin Walser set out his ideas of how the common bond ought to be preserved in the intellectual and cultural sphere for the long-term future and across all political boundaries, for the benefit of Germans in both countries.

We have, in my opinion, got beyond the period when our lives should be ruled by past catastrophes. We can already start trying to defend ourselves. We must not accept what has happened. But we can only succeed in taking countermeasures against what looks like fate if we are capable of allying ourselves with the march of history; if we acquire the ability to let the historical process work for us. For that, we must be obedient to it, but at the same time we must, to some degree, instil into it our own interests. . . .

If I were a German Academy, I would invite the nation's lyric poets to write a national anthem which, rather than performing an imaginary dance over lands conquered or to be conquered, would sketch out the landscape, the intellectual space in which the two Germanies can grow together.[22]

Yet surely here, too, any efforts by the Germans to achieve a greater sense of community across the dividing line must be firmly anchored in a Europe-wide process which promotes intellectual exchanges and cultural cooperation between the two halves of our continent. Forty years after 1945 and ten years after signature of the Helsinki Final Act, the CSCE Cultural Forum in Budapest, despite much

21. 'Drei Manifeste des ersten deutschen Schriftstellerkongresses 1947', quoted in K. Wagenbach et al. (eds.), *Vaterland, Muttersprache. Deutsche Schriftsteller und ihr Staat seit 1945*, Berlin, 1979, pp. 73f.
22. M. Walser, 'Über den Leser — soviel man in einem Festzelt sagen soll' (1978), quoted in H. Walwei-Wiegelmann (ed.), *Die Wunde namens Deutschland. Ein Lesebuch zur deutschen Teilung*, Freiburg/Heidelberg, 1981, pp. 316ff.

tension and discord, has sounded a few notes of hope. Among these was the idea, launched by Günther Grass, of an All-Europe Cultural Foundation. In his speech before the plenary session of the Cultural Forum, Andreas Meyer-Landrut, then Permanent Under-Secretary at the West German Foreign Office, made it clear that the FRG attaches great hopes to East–West cultural relations:

> It has already been shown in the past that cultural relations, like economic relations, represent a stabilising factor in international relationships, especially in times of tension and difficulty in political contacts. This arises not only from the fact that we can all recognise ourselves in the cultural offerings of others. The culture which Europe has shaped provides a bond so strong as to be the element which unites people across all the dividing lines in Europe. Shared ethnic and historical roots play a decisive role in this cultural area, in which we have no hesitation in including North America.[23]

23. A. Meyer-Landrut, 'Der Beitrag der Kultur zur Stabilisierung des Friedens', speech to the CSCE Cultural Forum, 25 November 1985, *Bulletin. Presse- und Informationsamt der Bundesregierung*, 134, p. 1175

Territory and population

Federal Republic of Germany including Berlin (West) according to states (Länder) and the GDR according to districts and Berlin (East).   As of 1 January 1984

The Federal Republic of Germany including Berlin (West) consists of eleven federal states. Its capital is Bonn (approx. 292,000 inhabitants) and the largest cities are Berlin (West), Hamburg and Munich, each of which has a population of more than one million. Cities with more than 500,000 are Cologne, Frankfurt/Main, Essen, Dortmund, Düsseldorf, Stuttgart, Duisburg, Bremen and Hanover.

In 1952 the states of Brandenburg, Mecklenburg, Saxony, Saxony-Anhalt and Thuringia in the GDR were redivided into 14 districts. The GDR regards Berlin (East), which has 1.2 million inhabitants, as an additional district and proclaimed it the capital – ignoring the fact that Berlin as a whole is under the authority of the four powers. Leipzig and Dresden, each with more than 500,000 inhabitants, are the two largest cities in the GDR. Cities with a population of over 100,000 are Karl-Marx-Stadt (formerly Chemnitz), Magdeburg, Rostock, Halle and Erfurt.

(In the case of the states of the Federal Republic of Germany, the sizes of territory and population differ slightly from previous statistics on account of boundary adjustments and cessions of territory that have taken place in the meantime.)

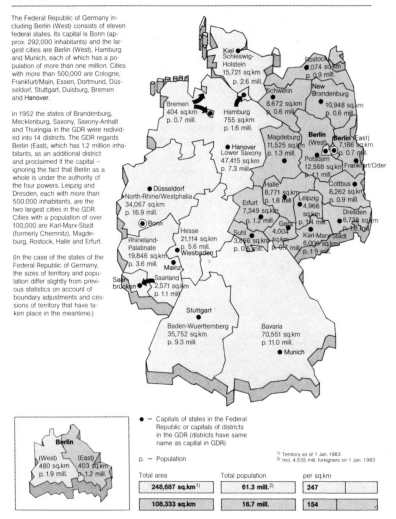

Kiel ●
Schleswig-Holstein
15,721 sq.km
p. 2.6 mill.

Rostock
9,074 sq.km
p. 0.9 mill.

Schwerin
Mecklenburg
8,672 sq.km
p. 0.6 mill.

New Brandenburg
10,948 sq.km
p. 0.6 mill.

Bremen
404 sq.km
p. 0.7 mill.

Hamburg
755 sq.km
p. 1.6 mill.

Magdeburg
11,525 sq.km
p. 1.3 mill.

Berlin (West)

Berlin (East)
7,186 sq.km
p. 0.7 mill.

● Hanover
Lower Saxony
47,415 sq.km
p. 7.3 mill.

Potsdam
12,568 sq.km
p. 1.1 mill.

Frankfurt/Oder

● Düsseldorf
North-Rhine/Westphalia
34,067 sq.km
p. 16.9 mill.

Halle
8,771 sq.km
p. 1.8 mill.

Cottbus ●
8,262 sq.km
p. 0.9 mill.

Erfurt
7,349 sq.km
p. 1.2 mill.

Leipzig
● 4,966 sq.km
p. 1.4 mill.

Dresden
● 6,738 sq.km
p. 1.8 mill.

● Bonn

Hesse
21,114 sq.km
p. 5.6 mill.
Wiesbaden ●

Suhl
3,856 sq.km
p. 0.5 mill.

Gera
4,004 sq.km
p. 0.7 mill.

Karl-Marx-Stadt
6,009 sq.km
p. 1.9 mill.

Rhineland-Palatinate
19,846 sq.km
p. 3.6 mill.
Mainz ●

Saarbrücken ●

Saarland
2,571 sq.km
p. 1.1 mill.

Stuttgart ●

Baden-Wuerttemberg
35,752 sq.km
p. 9.3 mill.

Bavaria
70,551 sq.km
p. 11.0 mill.

● Munich

● – Capitals of states in the Federal Republic or capitals of districts in the GDR (districts have same name as capital in GDR)

Berlin

(West)   (East)
480 sq.km   403 sq.km
p. 1.9 mill. p. 1.2 mill.

p. – Population

1) Territory as of 1 Jan. 1983
2) Incl. 4.535 mill. foreigners on 1 Jan. 1983

Total area	Total population	per sq.km
248,687 sq.km[1]	61.3 mill.[2]	247
108,333 sq.km	16.7 mill.	154

Source: Facts and Figures, p. 5

**Traffic routes
between Berlin (West) and the Federal Republic**

Border   Road   Waterway (Elbe)   Air corridor
Berlin Wall   Railway   Canal   Airport

Where the Elbe forms part of the border the course of the border has not
yet been determined.

Source: Facts and Figures, p. 121

6/German Questions — European Answers

What is the future of the German Question? Are there any practical prospects of development, or should one rather expect the reinforcement in the long-term of that status quo which has taken shape in the years since signature of the Basic Treaty between Bonn and East Berlin? Without doubt there is a serious contradiction between legitimate claims to self-determination and the realisation of the currently unalterable nature of postwar German division. This strikes hardest at the Germans in the GDR, of whom more is demanded as regards their acceptance of partition than is the case with their fellow-countrymen in the West. After more than a decade of efforts to normalise relations between the two Germanies, hopes of more freedom and human rights for all Germans remain fragile. Yet at the same time there is no convincing alternative in sight to direct dialogue and limited cooperation between two systems of society which by their very nature are irreconcilable.

Nothing in this 'normalisation' excludes finally the possibility of changes in the global political scene, shifts in power relationships between East and West, new forms of conflict or cooperation, or far-reaching changes in politics and society. Still unchanged is the fact that the relationship between the two Germanies remains not merely limited by the global antagonism between the superpowers, but threatened by it. From this the conclusion can be drawn that, in the last resort, the special problems of Germany cannot be acceptably solved in isolation but only within the context of a peace settlement for the whole of Europe.

The frontier which cuts through Berlin and Germany also runs through Europe; it divides the world. It follows that the two divisions, of Germany and of Europe, cannot be set off one against the other as in the power system of the nineteenth century, but can only be overcome together. Considered from the viewpoint that, as part of the global political confrontation since 1945, partitioning of countries has also been employed elsewhere as a diplomatic solution — one has only to think of Korea, Vietnam, Palestine — then this division appears in historical perspective as a new means of binding Germany into the whole European system of states, as often occurred in Germany's past. To that extent Germany's key role in and for Europe is nothing new, and Germany's neighbours have never ceased to see their own future as linked inseparably with that of the Germans. On the other hand, this insight into the conditions and limitations imposed by Europe upon German freedom of action also determined the decision of those who drafted the West German Constitution, to couple the achievement of German unity and freedom with the creation of a united Europe, in the preamble to the Basic Law.

The All-Europe Dimension of the German Question

The constant actuality of the German Question, sometimes latent, sometimes more open, within the Federal Republic, and in relations between the Germanies, and its periodic reemergence on the international scene, prompted the Faculty of Philosophy of the University of Augsburg to arrange an international conference in September 1981 on 'The German Question in the nineteenth and twentieth centuries'. In the introduction to the collected papers published two years later, the editors traced the functional dependence of the German problem upon international power relationships to a striking common denominator:

> The German Question — the complex of its territorial and national organisation, as well as the political, social, and economic situation in the area of *Mitteleuropa* settled by the Germans — this counts without doubt among the major problems of world history. In both the nineteenth and twentieth centuries, the solution of this problem has had a decisive influence on the balance of power, on leadership among the powers, and on hegemony over Europe; it has been decisive both for peace and for war on this continent and in the world. The German problem was a constitutive factor in the secular process by which 'Europe's world history' was allowed to lead into the old continent depriving itself of power. And its solution in the form of the European postwar order based on Potsdam and Helsinki appears today to have become the geopolitical core of a stable continental and global power balance and system of security under the dominance of the two hegemonial powers in this hemisphere.[1]

1. J. Becker and A. Hillgruber (eds.), *Die Deutsche Frage im 19. und 20. Jahrhundert*, Munich, 1983, p. viii

Papers and contributions to the discussion in the symposium make it clear once again that to look narrowly at the German Reich in the period since it was deprived of its powers in 1945 leads to two important facts being suppressed or overlooked: the European preconditions for solving the German Question, and the place held by it in the distinctive historical consciousness of neighbouring peoples.

Thinking based upon historical categories and their experiences with the people of Central Europe since the nineteenth century influenced the Allies in their planning both during and after the Second World War and still today to a large extent marks attitudes in the countries surrounding Germany. It is true that the right of the Germans to national self-determination may not be contested in principle by the allies and partners of the FRG, yet there are all kinds of fears that a nation-state consisting of the whole of Germany could once again attain an order of magnitude critical for Europe, and so destabilise the European regional system of the postwar period.

These two facts mean that, for the solution of the Germans' national problem today, forms of organisation have to be found which also take appropriate account of their neighbours' security interests. In concrete terms, this means that all working concepts for solving the German Question have to take as their starting point the basic preconditions of the international situation in order for them to become a reality; that not only must the Germans have the will to alter conditions in Europe's heartland, but they must be able to convince those around them that the model they propose as a solution would bring peace, security and other advantages to their neighbours also.

In a speech on the Day of German Unity, 17 June 1967, Chancellor Kiesinger, a Christian Democrat, put this basic dilemma as follows:

> Since we have to give thought to the German problem in all seriousness and honesty, we ought not to duck the question of how this lets us combine our policy of détente as a precondition for overcoming the division of our people, with our Western allegiance and with our efforts to unite Europe. Does the one not cancel out the other? Is this not where the tragic contradiction lies in the way we think and feel about our entire policy? Germany, a reunified Germany, would be of critically large size. It is too big not to have an effect on the balance of power, and too small to be able itself to hold the balance with the powers round about it. It is therefore in fact very hard to imagine that the whole of Germany could without further adjustment belong to one or other side, if the current

political structure in Europe continues. For this very reason, one can see the separate halves of Germany growing together only if this is firmly anchored in the process of overcoming the East-West conflict in Europe. . . . But what *is* possible is for us and those responsible in the other part of Germany to pursue discussions and agreements which would ease the difficulties created by the enforced division, and which ought to improve human, economic and intellectual contacts between the Germans. This should prevent the German people from drifting apart, year by year. This inner relaxation or detoxification would be in accordance with our grand design for the future peace of Europe; it could be very helpful to it.[2]

Just ten years later, President Scheel, who as foreign minister in the SPD–FDP coalition had had a decisive influence upon the *Ostpolitik* of the 1970s, made a statement on a similar occasion in the Bundestag:

The goal of German unity is frequently referred to with the word 'reunification'. At times the word is overlaid with a sense of restoration which I consider very problematical. We certainly do not want to get back to a state of political feeling, thought, and action which isolated our people in democratic Europe — of which Europe was fearful, since it had continually to watch out for irrational decisions as a result. We certainly do not want to get back to forms of government or types of state such as held power in the Germany of the Holy Roman Empire, the Wilhelmine Reich or, finally, the so-called 'Third Reich'.

Our struggle for unity is no dust-laden, backward-looking Reich-romanticism — unity is an aim directed towards peace in Europe in the future.

We strive for unity in order to 'serve the peace of the world as an equal partner in a united Europe'.

With these words of the Basic Law it becomes clear that the old-style nation-state, watching jealously over its sovereign rights, is not the objective of our struggle for unity . . . Germany will be one as a result of a long historical process. If it is realisable, history will present to us the forms which suit the times.[3]

These basic conditions of the *Deutschlandpolitik* have not changed to the present day. Forty years after the end of the war the Social

2. K.G. Kiesinger, 'Rede anlässlich des Staatsakts zum Tag der deutschen Einheit', 17 June 1967, quoted in B. Meissner (ed.), *Die deutsche Ostpolitik 1961–1970. Kontinuität und Wandel*, Cologne, 1970, pp. 206f.
3. W. Scheel, 'Rede am 25. Jahrestag des Tages der deutschen Einheit', 17 June 1978, quoted in H.W. Rubin (ed.), *Freiheit, Recht und Einigkeit. Zur Entspannungs- und Deutschlandpolitik der Liberalen*, Baden-Baden, 1980, pp. 38ff.

Democrat Vice-President of the Bundestag, Georg Leber, on the anniversary of the East Berlin uprising of 17 June 1953, underlined once more the European dimension of the German Question:

> The line of partition at the point reached by the armies in the Second World War, like a pitiless barrier between people, creates not only the division of our nation, it is also a pitiless barrier between the nations of Europe, for it cuts right across the common European cultural heritage which has grown up through a long European history. Therefore that makes the German Question also a part of the European Question. At the same time, what stands out clearly is that the German Question is not primarily a question of region, of territory or of frontiers. The German Question is in essence much more a matter of individual human rights, of human worth and self-determination.
>
> Since this is so, the German Question is also not a German quarrel in Europe, but part of Europe's plight, which will remain Europe's plight until that major part of Europe in which the values on which Europe was founded are now despised, becomes subject to a form of rule under which these values will be respected, for all people and thus for the whole of Europe.[4]

Building a European Peace Order

The connection between the German Question and the future organisation of Europe has time and again for over forty years provoked strong controversy and critical enquiry, but also a wealth of working hypotheses, such as the uniting of the whole of Europe for the peaceful overcoming of East–West tensions. Certainly that should not make one lose sight of the fact that the idea of a solution to European peace problems for the time being is nothing more than a vague vision, the practical realisation of which seems just as far away as the dream of German unity. Nothing much is likely to alter there, either, so long as the realities of political control in Eastern Europe offer only very limited opportunities for a peaceful reshaping of the pattern of postwar Europe.

Until well into the 1950s all seemed still to be in a state of flux. There were still sufficient grounds for thinking that, as a result of global political developments, a democratic German core-state in the West would sooner or later draw the Eastern half of the country also into the sphere of the free world. Thus Chancellor Adenauer, a

4. G. Leber, 'Rede zum Gedenken an den 17. Juni 1953', 17 June 1985, in *Bulletin. Presse- und Informationsamt der Bundesregierung*, 68, 1985, pp. 571f.

few days after the foundation of the German Democratic Republic, could declare in the West German Bundestag to lengthy and enthusiastic applause by the right and centre parties and the SPD:

> We are convinced that our epoch, often seemingly so hopeless, will lead in the end to a fruitful rebuilding of the political and international order, the order which will have grown out of the soil of equal rights for all. Our foremost aim will be to unite all Germany on the basis of justice and freedom and to introduce it into a European framework.[5]

Only when Adenauer refused to be drawn into the Soviet exchange of notes of 1952 or to press the Western powers to sound out Soviet readiness to compromise in new Four Power negotiations, did the *Deutschlandpolitik* followed by the Chancellor diverge from that of the Social Democrat opposition. Soviet motives and Western reactions to the Stalin Note of 10 March 1952 and subsequent Notes from the Kremlin are still debated hotly to this day. The proposal made at that time was on the lines of an armed but neutral united Germany, in which no one was seriously interested, bar a small minority. The West's counter-proposal was for free elections and freedom of action for an all-German government. This would have made possible the integration of the whole of Germany into the West, which Stalin by his offer had already tried to prevent for the Federal Republic.

The positions of East and West were thus from the beginning irreconcilable. In particular, Konrad Adenauer considered a neutralised and united Germany between the two power blocs as the first step towards a Soviet take-over in the whole of Germany; he therefore called for absolute priority to be given to securing democracy in the Federal Republic through Western integration. The much-used phrase 'missed opportunities' of 1952, shows that what we are dealing with here is for the Germans an unresolved, central problem, which through retrospective interpretation and the creation of legends has long been divorced from practical historical realities. Like the Yalta conference of February 1945, of which the actual political events were very far removed from the historical myth of a 'division of the world', the Stalin Note of 1952 is among those themes on which German national frustrations are focused, even today. What turned upon that decision of the 1950s was that neither the integration of Western Europe, nor the later reunification of Germany expected to result from a 'policy of strength', was

---

5. K. Adenauer, 'Erklärung vor dem Bundestag', 21 October 1949, quoted in Auswärtiges Amt (eds.), *Die Auswärtige Politik*, pp. 157ff.

achieved. Looking back from the vantage point of 1985, Heinrich Windelen, the then Christian Democrat Minister for Intra-German Relations, has justified the way the course was set at that time:

> The Soviet advance through Central Europe as far as the Elbe was seen by Adenauer as *the* absolutely epoch-making event. The consequence which he drew from that for the nation was to act as follows: to ensure the liberty and independence of that part of the nation which by grace of history and geography had been saved from seizure by the Soviets.
>
> This priority in *Deutschlandpolitik* is today no less appropriate to the real situation of Germany than in Konrad Adenauer's time. It is fulfilled by the deliberate choice of values of freedom and self-determination which do not place unity of the nation-state above all else. . . . The preeminence given to freedom and self-determination before unity allows forms of solution for the German problem which go beyond the re-establishment of the nation-state.[6]

With the conclusion of the Germany Treaty in 1954, Adenauer succeeded in establishing in treaty form the support of the three Western powers for his concept of 'unity in freedom', yet the chances of this proposition being realised grew markedly less as a result of the fixing of the European status quo. In this situation, the Chancellor decided to maintain unaltered both the political strategy and the legal position regarding Germany's future, at the same time, however, giving thought in his policy planning to unconventional attempts at a solution. The surprising suggestion of an 'Austrian status' for the GDR, which Adenauer asked the Soviet Ambassador Smirnov to consider in March 1958, probably arose from some basic thinking which had gone on in the Chancellor's office in regard to the negotiations in Moscow in September 1955.

With these ideas there already existed in outline the *Deutschlandpolitik* which, in the latter part of the 1960s, envisaged an institutionalised *modus vivendi* with the GDR and the countries of Eastern Europe, and no longer aimed at setting in motion the process of reunification in the short- or medium-term. Yet, until his departure from the political stage, Adenauer preferred to be seen to pursue the former course. Public discussion about the actual shape of a European peace order began at the level of government only with the

6. H. Windelen, 'Dreissig Jahre Deutschlandvertrag. Rede vor der Deutschen Sektion der Europäischen Konferenz für Menschenrechte und Selbstbestimmung in Bonn', 24 April 1985', in *Informationen. Bundesminister für innerdeutsche Beziehungen*, 9, 1985, p. 15

creation of the Grand Coalition between the CDU-CSU and SPD in 1966. Willy Brandt, then Foreign Minister, gave his basic ideas on this question when he was interviewed on West Germany's radio service:

> A European peace order should not be seen . . . as if it was simply a matter of confirming what the Second World War left behind in Europe. The European peace order ought to level out the barriers and make new forms of cooperation possible. For example, it should include a European law to protect ethnic minorities. It ought not simply to proclaim human rights, but to practise them in essential areas. A European peace order also means, finally, an economic alliance, that is, via bilateral trade relations between East and West, the EEC and Comecon would be brought together in a workable association.[7]

The key to such a peaceful order in Europe was considered to be the relationship between the two halves of Germany. No answer was given to the question of the form in which it would be possible for all Germans to live together within the context of the new peace order. What was clearly expressed, however, was that no matter how strong the desire for reconciliation and cooperation, the principles of liberty and democracy could in no way be sacrificed. The Liberal Ralf Dahrendorf, at that time Parliamentary Under-Secretary in the Bonn Foreign Office, speaking in April 1970 before the Council of Europe, denied that behind this concept stood the assumption that there must come about a gradual convergence between the political systems: 'In our view there must and shall be no middle course for the Western democracies between freedom and lack of freedom. There must and shall also be no compromise between the liberal and communist social orders'.[8]

In the mid-1960s leading politicians of the Western alliance had similarly acted on the assumption that a reunification of Germany would only be possible at the end of a lengthy process of rapprochement between East and West. The French President, Charles de Gaulle, gave an important impetus to the thinking behind Bonn's *Ostpolitik* at the beginning of 1965, with his ideas of a 'Europeanising of the German Question'. The General advanced the view that the German problem could only be solved through the involvement of all

7. W. Brandt, 'Grundvorstellungen einer europäischen Friedensordnung', interview on *Deutschlandfunk*, 2 June 1967, quoted in Haftendorn et al., *Die Aussenpolitik*, p. 327
8. R. Dahrendorf, 'Rede vor der Beratenden Versammlung des Europarats', 22 April 1970, quoted in *Texte zur Deutschlandpolitik*, vol. V, Bonn, 1973, p. 38

neighbouring countries after the whole of Europe 'from the Atlantic to the Urals' had rediscovered its unity. As a precondition for this, however, the Soviet Union must cease to be a totalitarian state, and the East European countries would have to be able to act independently. At the same time, de Gaulle left no doubt that he considered necessary the recognition of the Oder–Neisse line and a definite renunciation of atomic weapons. The European dimensions of the German Question were presented by him as follows:

> The German problem is the European problem *par excellence*. European — just think back — since the emergence of the Roman Empire, that is, since Europe ceased historically to be limited to the shores of the Mediterranean, in order to extend as far as the Rhine; European, because the areas settled by the Teutons in the heart of our continent lay in between the Gauls, the Latins and the Slavs; European, because in the course of a long and difficult history, it was burdened with many upheavals, many fateful consequences which have left behind throughout the centuries bitter resentment and much prejudice among all neighbouring peoples against this country which was in the throes of an eternal becoming. It is a European problem, because the German people is a great people in the field of economics and also of the intellect, science, and the arts, as well as in the sphere of military capability, and because Europe sees in it an essential part of itself; European, too, because Germany has always been filled with anxiety and at times with anger — born out of its own insecurity regarding its frontiers, its unity, its political order and international role — and therefore its fate continues to appear to the whole continent as all the more worrying, the longer it remains uncertain. . . .
>
> So the problem is posed anew against the background of history. For France, everything can be summarised in three closely interconnected observations: that we have to act so that Germany becomes a sure factor for progress and peace; to contribute, on this condition, to its reunification; to pursue the path and to choose the framework which will make this possible.[9]

While, in de Gaulle's conception, the reunification of Germany was still an integral part of his vision of a future Europe, the formula for Europeanising the German Question employed by the CSU Chairman Franz Josef Strauss since 1965 (see his book *The Grand Design*) was an altogether too revolutionary viewpoint for contemporary minds. By describing the nation-state as a quasi-anachronistic image, he suggested to the Germans that they should give up their

---

9. C. de Gaulle, 'Conférence de presse du 4 février 1965', in *Discours et Messages*, pt. IV, Paris, 1970, pp. 35f.

out-dated efforts at reunification in favour of creating a region of Greater Europe.

> Since the German people live in the middle of a Europe which is divided politically and ideologically, they ought not to waste their energies in striving for restoration of the nation-state, which even theoretically would only be thinkable with unsatisfactory limitations, but which basically would neither correspond to the general course of developments, nor would encourage it. . . .
>
> If they understood that the nation-state represents a survival from the past which can no longer serve the peoples of Europe as a strong-hold for their self-determination, their prosperity and their further intellectual development, it would be easy for the Germans to decide to see the chief aim of their national interest in the creation of a region of Greater Europe in which, too, it would again be possible for their nation to live together with others in a natural way.[10]

Klaus Bloemer, at that time Strauss's adviser on foreign policy, was considerably clearer on the practical form which a European peace order would take in order to guarantee the German potential being built up as an organic part of the whole European construction, while at the same time taking into account the natural interests of the Germans and their neighbours:

> The 'Europeanising of the German Question' ought not to degenerate into a fashionable political catch phrase. Over-worked slogans, which some people use to conceal their harping on a repetitive set of ideas, and with which others seem to escape from uncomfortable and potentially unpopular consequences, are quite common enough in national and international politics. Someone who says that A is necessary for over-coming the division of Europe should not shy away from the B of decisions needed on the political plane in Western Europe, which in turn make unavoidable changes to the existing structure of the Western alliance. But in reality both A and B belong with the C of personally coming to terms with the fact of two German states; this should be understood as a conscious and active first step towards a solution based on an all-European community, a Community of Greater Europe. The other way round produces no solution which the other Europeans would accept. In other words, we would simply be accused of wanting to Germanise the European question instead of Europeanising the German one.[11]

10. F.-J. Strauss, 'Nation mit neuem Auftrag. Die Einheit der Deutschen im geeinten Europa', in *Die politische Meinung*, 2–3, 1967, pp. 13ff.
11. K. Bloemer, 'Die Europäisierung der Deutschen Frage im Geiste kooperativer

Some ten years later, a French expert on Germany, Henri Ménudier, came to very similar conclusions. In his closing remarks in a platform discussion on 'German unity — hope, nightmare, or illusion?' he said:

> It is quite right to be thinking of eventual solutions, in case one day there should be some movement on the German question. I fear that the Germans are far too introspective about it, and do not give enough thought to the ideas of citizens of the GDR or the reservations of neighbouring states. Discussions like this show just how much difficulty the citizens of the Federal Republic have with their identity. They have built a fine country (the FRG), but all they can think about is abandoning it or enlarging it! Like married men who are constantly looking back at their former adventures or thinking about the chances they are currently missing with other women! A sign of the eternal German restlessness?
>
> The Germans should entertain no illusory hopes, so that German unity cannot again become a nightmare for Europe.[12]

Forty Years On: What Germany's Neighbours Would Like

'To be German is to have a difficult fate', wrote Friedrich Sieburg more than fifty years ago in an essay on the Germans and the world:

> The eyes of the entire world are turned upon us from all sides, like gun barrels trained on the condemned man's chest or binoculars on a dark cloud on the horizon. None look with indifference. . . . We have the uncanny powers of attraction of a grenade found in an open field. Has it exploded already, or is it about to go off? Above all, *when* will it go off?[13]

In many respects this comment is valid even today yet, unlike then, there is surely no German politician who would be proud of the fact that other people are at times uncertain whether they are dealing here with a dud or a time fuse. The baffling thing in the present situation seems rather to be that the rest of the world in nearly every respect believes the Germans capable of more than they do themselves.

Many foreign reactions to the reawakened debate about the German Question have in recent times reaffirmed how deeply the

Koexistenz. Gastvorlesung am Otto Suhr-Institut der Freien Universität Berlin', 5 February 1968, in *Die politische Information*, March 1968 (special issue), p. 8

12. H. Ménudier, *Das Deutschlandbild der Franzosen in den 70er Jahren*, Bonn, 1981, p. 68
13. F. Sieburg, *Es werde Deutschland*, Frankfurt a.Main, 1933, p. 55

past has marked people's consciousness, and how easily the underlying anxieties can break out again. In a contribution to a series of
articles published by *Die Zeit*, entitled 'The 8th May Commemoration: a Hurdle to be Crossed,' the Prague-born historian Saul
Friedländer, who works in Tel Aviv and Geneva, expressed his own
fears:

> A new nationalism is emerging in Germany, on the right and on the left.
> For some it is a matter of a perfectly ordinary search for identity, but with
> others it is a case of the expression of not entirely harmless longings. . . .
>
> One has the impression that there is once again that old conflict in
> Germany between culture and civilisation, and the Germans — at any
> rate, so far as their attitudes and longings are concerned, perhaps not
> their political options — are ridding themselves bit by bit of the 're-
> education' forced upon them by the Allies and are seeking independent
> expressions of their national feeling. . . .
>
> Between the Germany of today and its watchful observers there exists a
> bond of magnanimity. This bond is fragile. Its dissolution would rep-
> resent the victory, from beyond the grave, of the most terrible thing that
> mankind has ever produced.[14]

For Alfred Grosser, a Frenchman born in Frankfurt, the Federal
Republic of Germany has even more ethical obligations than other
countries, because it originated not as a nation, but on the basis of
the rejection of totalitarianism and the affirmation of the Western
understanding of democracy:

> At the core is the concept of freedom. This applies first of all to Berlin,
> which suddenly, in June 1948, from being the symbol of the Third Reich,
> became the symbol of freedom, and thus hastened — and even made
> possible — the rise of West Germany to being an equal partner. In two
> respects, that cannot be said often enough to the peace movement and to
> some intellectuals of the Left. In Berlin, liberty has been preserved since
> 1948 thanks to the reciprocal nuclear threat. That shows that this threat
> can be useful, provided that one wants to protect the Berliners' liberty, a
> point not very often mentioned in and by the German peace movement.
> Certainly it is right to dismantle false images of the enemy. But that ought
> not to mean that one ceases to point out the basic difference between the
> idea of freedom and the reality of freedom. . . .
>
> Hitler was an historical fact. So was the total deprivation of Germany's

14. S. Friedländer, 'Bewältigung — oder nur Verdrängung? Bei der deutschen Suche
    nach der Identität kann die Geschichte auf der Strecke bleiben', in *Die Zeit*, 8
    February 1985

power in 1945. Then came a little later the division, which did not arise directly from the deprivation of power. No other country is so marked by its past as the Federal Republic. It is therefore not just a normal state like others. As an economic power and as a democracy it is a pillar of the West, to which it belongs, even if it is only part of a nation. Its partners have to live with this contradiction as well. The more openly and honestly the Germans do so themselves, the easier it will be for their partners, too.[15]

The American historian Gordon Craig, for his part, insisted in his *Zeit* article on the need to renew a personal commitment to peace, and wanted to see the 8 May understood as a challenge to the Germans to approach their history in a more pragmatic way:

[It would] naturally be foolish to expect today's generation to feel any kind of personal responsibility for actions carried out in Germany's name during the years 1939 to 1945. But an understanding that these actions *were* carried out is important above all because there are groups today in the FRG who have apparently so suppressed all memories of the war, that they do not hesitate to make speeches calling for Germany's historic right to territories which were lost through the war. This is a serious denial of memory and can only be corrected through permanent reminders of the fact that the crimes of the Hitler regime were real crimes, which actually took place, and that the measures of retaliation by the victims and their descendants were the logical consequences of this.

In fact, it seems appropriate that the 8 May should be understood as an invitation to the Germans to approach their history more pragmatically than hitherto. They have always found this difficult: they have preferred instead — as already pointed out by Heine and Nietzsche — to reinterpret their history, to idealise it, to make of it a vehicle for visions of the future and not infrequently to use it as a weapon against certain aspects of the present which they find uncomfortable.[16]

It is surely no accident that Nietzsche's famous definition of the German character has recently reappeared very frequently in connection with analyses of the 'German unrest'. Explaining the effect which the Overture to *The Mastersinger of Nuremberg* had on him, Nietzsche at one point described Wagner's music as eloquently symbolising a certain German tendency towards suffering in the present:

15. A. Grosser, 'Mit dem Widerspruch leben. Der Begriff der Befreiung sollte über die Fixierung auf die Vergangenheit hinweghelfen', in *Die Zeit*, 1 March 1985
16. G. Craig, 'Eine Selbstverpflichtung für den Frieden. Der Jahrestag des Kriegsendes sollte wirklich ein Tag der Erinnerung sein und niemandes Gefühle schonen', in *Die Zeit*, 22 March 1985

... something German in the best and worst sense of the word, something in the German style, manifold, formless, and inexhaustible ... a real, genuine token of the German soul, which is at the same time young and aged, too ripe and yet still too rich in futurity. This kind of music expresses best what I think of the Germans: they belong to the day before yesterday and the day after tomorrow — *they have as yet no today*.[17]

The Berliner Peter Schneider's 'wall jumper' seems to be an example of this from recent times. These people cross the frontier Wall repeatedly in both directions, without ever finding what they are really looking for. They jump across the dividing line between two unloved social systems without a true homeland and they will not commit themselves to either. This author makes clear, too, the ambivalence of the diffuse sense of unease at the current state of the German nation, when he writes of both halves of Germany: 'In their pain at separation, they resemble a lover who sorrows less for the loss of his loved one than for the strong feelings that he once had'.[18]

So it is only an apparent paradox that pacifists and neutralists who consider themselves the most peace-loving and undangerous of Germans are regarded, at least in other countries of the West, as nationalists — although there are similar movements in some other NATO countries. For 'nationalist' here does not stand for the motives, but for the effects of their behaviour, and these are seen as generally threatening, if the Germans were to get on the move again, because they feel spiritually and politically without a homeland. It is not the initial question of where they would move to which arouses suspicion, but simply the fact of movement, the restlessness, the lack of resolution or repose.

A colloquium was held in the Berlin Reichstag building in December 1983, arranged jointly by the Franco-German Institute of Ludwigsburg and the Centre for Information and Research on Contemporary Germany (CIRAC) of Paris; the theme was 'Germany in Europe. A Question of National Identity'. The former editor of the journal *Esprit*, Paul Thibaud, voiced some harsh criticism of tendencies towards 'the denial of politics' and 'the abandonment of history', in connection with the German search for identity:

I personally want to say to you quite frankly that to me this seems morbid and negative, that this kind of self-questioning has to be got over precisely because it comes down to the fact that this question of identity is being

17. F. Nietzsche, *Jenseits von Gut und Böse*, transl. Helen Zimmern
18. P. Schneider, *Der Mauerspringer*, Darmstadt/Neuwied, 1984, p. 27

posed in the political sphere as a problem of authenticity, of self-fulfilment, of inner truth, of subjectivity, of the primacy of personal experience. But this is a denial of the true nature of politics. This kind of subjective thinking can be found for instance in the ecology movement and in certain forms of demand to run one's own affairs, it is a kind of hyper-inflation of the ego, to which the outside world appears as insult, violation, aggression. But this view of politics is inimical to policies for freedom. . . .

What is paradoxical is the attitude of the Germans towards NATO. Ninety per cent speak out in opinion polls for staying in NATO, yet at the same time many are against NATO decisions. This means that they feel their own views are being disregarded by an organisation which they expect first and foremost to serve their own interests and satisfy German narcissism. Such a surface appearance of modest subservience is truly egocentric, one of those strange psycho-political problems that one particularly comes across in Germany.[19]

Contradictions of another kind were diagnosed by the Pole, Ryszard Wojna, Chairman of the Foreign Policy Committee of the Sejm, in a platform discussion at the 21st German Protestant Church congress in Düsseldorf in June 1985, under the heading 'Reconciliation between Neighbours — Wishes for the Future'. Against the background of differences of opinion emerging at the beginning of 1985 within the CDU-CSU in the Bundestag over the Warsaw Treaty of 1970 and the current status of the (formerly German) Eastern regions, Wojna gave expression to anxieties shared by many of his fellow-countrymen that Poland's territorial integrity might be questioned again in the context of a future settlement of the German Question:

In my opinion there was never in the past simply one German identity. To the question: 'What is the Fatherland to a German?' — and Fatherland is not just a material term — there were always many different answers. Today many of the answers to this question even contain internal contradictions. . . . I ask myself: How can one be at the same time a European and someone who does not want to recognise the frontiers now existing in Europe?[20]

19. P. Thibaud, contribution to discussion at the Franco-German colloquium 'Deutschland in Europa. Fragen an die nationale Identität', 15–17 December 1983, quoted in R. Picht, 'Frankreich und die deutsche Identität. Ein Berliner Gespräch über Deutschlands Platz und Rolle in Europa', *Dokumente*, 2, 1984, p. 106
20. R. Wojna, '40 Jahre danach. Versöhnung mit den Nachbarn: Wünsche für die Zukunft', in *Deutscher Evangelischer Kirchentag Düsseldorf 1985. Dokumente*, Stuttgart, 1985, p. 411

Utterances of this kind show clearly how hard it is even forty years after the end of the war to find understanding for the national problems of the Germans. The FRG has repeatedly stressed its understanding for Polish claims to existence as a state within secure borders but cannot, on the other hand, anticipate a peace settlement by giving up the German and Western legal position. For the CDU–CSU parliamentary group, its spokesman on foreign policy and deputy chairman, Volker Rühe, set out the basis of Bonn's policy in a Bundestag debate at the beginning of 1985, with the express support of Chancellor Kohl:

> We have understanding for the wish of the Polish people to live within secure frontiers and in a state which is territorially viable. The Federal Republic of Germany took account of these justified interests of the Polish people in the Warsaw Treaty. In so doing it could only act legally in its own name and could not anticipate a peace treaty. That is the legal position.
>
> There is also, however, a political position. Anyone who reflects soberly and without illusion will know that the Warsaw Treaty with Poland had a politically binding effect which also could not be ignored by a reunited Germany. . . . Anyone who wants a European peace order in which frontiers lose their political significance — which is what we all want — must also know that only frontiers which are not politically disputed can lose their significance.[21]

In a comprehensive inquiry into the international and historical dimensions of the German Question, Eberhard Schulz, Deputy Director of the Research Institute of the German Association for Foreign Policy in Bonn, referred a few years ago to the fact that the official position of the FRG, not only towards its Eastern neighbours, but also in relation to Western Alliance partners, called for some clarification, since in certain circumstances it could even hamper progress on the road to political integration within the European Community:

> Basing the FRG's existence upon the continuation of the German Reich in its 1937 borders — however abstract an idea and meant only as a tactical negotiating position for possible peace negotiations — does in fact also imply that the Federal Republic might actually try to reestablish the German Reich in its 1937 frontiers. But if it succeeded in bringing together in one state the potential power within this territory, and then

---

21. V. Rühe 'Rede in der Aktuellen Stunde des Bundestags', 6 February 1985, in *Das Parlament* 7–8, 1985, p. 11

brought it into the European Community, the other member states would probably see that as a position of political and economic hegemony for Germany.

So long as a development of this kind cannot exclude such probabilities, the FRG's partners in the Community have an additional reason for pursuing the course towards political integration very cautiously. This is all the more true, as the impression created by the policy of keeping open the·frontier question, that the Germans could still raise some claim to the Oder–Neisse region, involves the FRG in a lasting conflict with Moscow and Warsaw and drives the Poles ever more firmly into the arms of the Soviets. This is a conflict which the West Europeans are unwilling to be drawn into.[22]

The Germans' Responsibility to Europe

At the commemoration in the German parliament of the fortieth anniversary of the ending of the war in Europe and of the National Socialist tyranny the President of the FRG, Richard von Weizsäcker, in vivid words urged that 'there is every reason for us to recognise 8 May 1945 as the end of an aberration in German history, an end bearing seeds of hope for a better future'. From this recognition the Germans had a special obligation to make their contribution to a peaceful order in Europe, through the renunciation of force and the will for understanding:

> Renouncing force today means giving people lasting security, unchallenged on political grounds, for their future in the place where fate drove them after the 8th May and where they have been living in the decades since. It means placing the dictate of understanding above conflicting legal claims. That is the true, human contribution to a peaceful order in Europe which we can provide. . . .
>
> Peace and good neighbourly relations with all countries should radiate from the German soil in both States. And no other states should let that soil become a source of danger to peace either. The people of Germany are united in desiring a peace that encompasses justice and human rights for all peoples, including our own. Reconciliation that transcends boundaries cannot be provided by a walled Europe but only by a continent that removes the divisive elements from its borders. That is the exhortation given us by the end of the Second World War.[23]

22. E. Schulz, *Die deutsche Nation in Europa. Internationale und historische Dimensionen*, Bonn, 1982, pp. 204f.
23. R.v. Weizsäcker, 'Der 8. Mai 1945 — 40 Jahre danach', in *Von Deutschland aus. Reden des Bundespräsidenten*, Berlin, 1985, pp. 13ff.

If one considers the task laid down in the Basic Law in the light of realities described in this way, then the 'achievement of unity' appears to be, before all else, a matter of aiming at personal liberties not the shifting of frontiers. The European people can survive only in a peaceful order which ensures that countries with differing political systems can live together, without making changes in those systems a prerequisite. Accordingly, political efforts must concentrate on the gradual transcending of the divisive character of the frontiers which split Europe. The overcoming of division understood in this way does not exclude the reunification of the two German states with the agreement of all European neighbours and all allies. Overcoming division can also mean, however, supporting an 'Austrian solution' for liberalising the GDR, in the sense once under consideration by Adenauer, without necessarily calling in question its membership of the Warsaw Pact.

The necessity of speaking out for overcoming the separation caused by the barriers between sytems becomes still more pressing because of the existence of the city of Berlin. The saying coined there, that 'the German Question remains open so long as the Brandenburg Gate is shut', strikes at the heart of the problem. Berlin forces the two German states into political contact with each other and repeatedly requires both the FRG and the GDR to speak out strongly within their respective alliances for the removal of tensions. The Berlin crises during the Cold War, the dangers stirred up because of this for peace in Europe and world-wide, are historic proof of this. The Social Democrat Hans Apel, his party's candidate at the Berlin elections in 1985, has put as follows the close connection between Berlin and policies on Germany:

> But one cannot expect the West Berliners to put up with the current situation. What they want is long-term reconciliation with their environment, without forfeiting their internal and external freedoms and the ties with the Federal Republic and the West. That means reestablishing the multiplicity of contacts which any major town has with its surrounding hinterland. Only this could lead to a real normalisation of Berlin's situation.
>
> The decisive step in this cannot be taken by West Berlin alone, in its own strength, and it does require support through the policies of the Bonn Government and by the powers which guarantee Berlin's status. For Berlin there is no acceptable alternative to present policies on Germany. Berlin compels all the powers involved in this part of the world to get on with each other here, peacefully, and compels the FRG above all not to allow its relationship with the GDR to deteriorate.[24]

Forty years after the war's end the political scientist Hans-Peter Schwarz undertook a critical examination of the foreign policy style which he described as that of 'tamed Germans'. Efforts to balance out international contradictions and to bring reconciliation to neighbouring people are described by him as setting the basic style of West German foreign policy. The first half century he saw as marked by a German 'obsession with power', while the policy of the Federal Republic could be characterised more as 'forgetfulness of power'. If the Germans had a dream role, it was that of harmonisation and peace-making:

> The effort at harmonisation is not only a reaction against the excesses of a still not too far distant past. It not only gives expression to the precarious state of international security. It is in large part conditioned by the wide-ranging interests of a world trading nation. Like all industrialised countries of Western Europe, the FRG also sees itself caught up inescapably in a network of world-wide and regional interdependences. Interdependence offers a wide range of positive opportunities for the future, but at the same time it makes us dependent, even helpless. We can do nothing against it, we can only try to adopt a style of behaviour appropriate to the system. This does not lead to a clear national image, but it does lead to external economic relations being kept as tension-free as possible.[25]

The collapse of 1945 and the exposed security position of Germany in the heart of Europe have helped this mental attitude, found generally in liberal societies, to get established in the FRG. Additionally, in the area of trade with the East there is the view, current mainly since the 1970s, that the economic dimension of East–West relations should be regarded to a certain extent as a confidence-building measure in the sense contained in the Helsinki Final Act. Thus the Bonn Foreign Minister, Hans-Dietrich Genscher, declared in the Bundestag in September 1984, and with the full support of the FDP, the CDU-CSU, and the SPD:

> When we ratified here the long-term German–Soviet economic agreement, I protested, as Foreign Minister of the government of that time, against seeing the significance of this agreement primarily in terms of the economic opportunities. As I said then: Those are there, too, but of first importance is the fact that long-term economic cooperation provides a bit

24. H. Apel, 'Deutschland-Politik — Möglichkeiten und Grenzen', in *Europa-Archiv*, 20, 1984, pp. 615f.
25. H.-P. Schwarz, *Die gezähmten Deutschen. Von der Machtbesessenheit zur Machtvergessenheit*, Stuttgart, 1985, p. 33

of confidence-building between West and East. You ought to recognise this political component. Only if we do this on a broad plane do we create ever-stronger joint interests — here I should like to bring in a word often heard in the East — interests which make a policy irreversible, a policy of which we believe that it must lead in the direction of a European peace order.[26]

The Federal Parliamentary elections of January 1987 proved once again that West German democracy as a political system can resist both the temptations of nationalism and the lure of Utopian idealism. The integration of the Federal Republic in the European Community has reduced, at least for the Western part of the country, some of the uncertainties traditionally associated with Germany's location at the crossroads between East and West. The ties which have developed between the Federal Republic and Western Europe, on ideological, political, economic and military levels, cannot be undone and render extremely unlikely any return to traditional see-saw policies between East and West.

Interdependence creates ties and obligations. It forms a basis for cooperation, but also for situations of conflict, chiefly because it gives rise to new vulnerabilities. European Community solidarity provides a regulator and guards against the risk of the partners drifting apart, but it can also make it difficult at times for all the members to accept each other's differences. At the beginning of 1948, in the early stages of Franco-German reconciliation, the poet and diplomat Paul Claudel saw an urgent need to give back to Germany 'that inestimable benefit of which no Christian people should be deprived: the right to a future, the right to hope'. His words carry deep significance even today, with their reminder that German responsibilities towards Europe cannot be dissociated from European responsibilities towards Germany:

Germany has need of Europe and Europe has need of the Germans. This is not just a matter for 'them': it is a matter for 'us'. Madame de Sévigné used to say that she was suffering from her daughter's sore throat. So long as Germany continues in its present situation, Europe will suffer from Germany's sickness and will fail to recover its true balance. . . .

France's role is to understand. Why should Germany's role not be to create consensus, in the true meaning of the word? To arouse in all the nations which surround it a mutual sense of their need for one another?[27]

26. H.-D. Genscher, 'Debatte zur Deutschlandpolitik', 12 September 1984, in *Informationen. Bundesministerium für innerdeutsche Beziehungen*, 18, 1984, p. 52
27. P. Claudel, 'Quelques réflexions sur l'Allemagne', 8 March 1948, in idem, *Oeuvres en prose*, Paris, 1965, pp. 1385ff.

Chronology

1943

14–25 June	Casablanca Conference (Roosevelt, Churchill)
28 Nov.–1 Dec.	Tehran Conference (Roosevelt, Stalin, Churchill)

1944

12 Sept.	Protocol of the European Advisory Commission on the division of Germany into zones
14 Nov.	Decisions of the European Advisory Commission on the control machinery in Germany

1945

4–11 Feb.	Yalta Conference (Roosevelt, Stalin, Churchill)
7/8 May	Unconditional surrender of German forces at Rheims and Berlin-Karlshorst
5 June	Declaration of the defeat of Germany and the assumption of supreme authority by the victorious powers
17 July–2 August	Potsdam Conference (Truman, Churchill, then Attlee, Stalin)

1946

21/22 Apr.	Forced amalgamation of KPD and SPD in Soviet zone to form SED
25 Apr.–15 May 15 June–12 July	Foreign Ministers' Conference of victorious powers in Paris

1947

1 Jan.	Economic administration in American and British zones combined (Bizonia)
10 Mar.–24 Apr.	Foreign Ministers' Conference in Moscow
6–9 June	Conference of German *Land* Prime Ministers in Munich
25 Nov.–15 Dec.	Foreign Ministers' Conference in London

1948

24 June	Start of the Berlin Blockade
1 August	French zone of occupation joined to the Bizone to form one economic area (Trizone)

1949

4 April	Establishment of NATO
12 May	End of the Berlin Blockade
23 May	Basic Law of the Federal Republic of Germany (FRG)

	comes into force
23 May–20 June	Foreign Ministers' Conference in Paris
21 Sept.	Occupied status comes into effect
7 October	Establishment of the German Democratic Republic (GDR)

1950

9 May	Robert Schuman proposes European Coal and Steel Community (ECSC)
25 June	Start of the Korean War
5 August	Charter of the Germans expelled from their home-lands (*Heimatvertriebenen*)
26 October	René Pleven proposes formation of a European army with participation by the FRG

1951

15 March	Re-establishment of the (West) German Foreign Office
18 April	Signing of the European Coal and Steel Community Treaty in Paris
20 September	Interzonal Trade Agreement between the FRG and East German authorities

1952

10 Mar.–23 Sept.	Exchange of Notes between the Soviet Union and Western powers over a Peace Treaty with Germany
26 May	Signing of the Germany Treaty in Bonn between the FRG and the three Western Allies
27 May	Signing of the European Defence Community (EDC) Treaty in Paris

1953

| 17 June | Popular uprising in the GDR and East Berlin |

1954

25 Jan.–18 Feb.	Foreign Ministers' Conference of the Four Powers in Berlin
25 March	The GDR acquires further sovereignty rights
23 October	Western Allies end occupation (Germany Treaty)

1955

25 January	Soviet Union declares the ending of the state of war with Germany
5 May	The FRG regains its sovereignty under the Paris Treaty
9 May	The FRG joins NATO
14 May	Founding of the Warsaw Pact (GDR a member)
17–23 July	Geneva Summit Conference (Eisenhower, Bulganin, Eden, Faure)

| 9–13 Sept. | Visit by Chancellor Adenauer to Moscow: resumption of diplomatic relations with USSR |
| 17–20 Sept. | GDR Premier Grotewohl in Moscow: GDR acquires sovereignty |

1956

| 18 January | Founding of East German National People's Army |
| 7 July | West German Parliament passes military conscription law |

1957

| 25 March | Signing of Rome Treaties forming the EEC and Euratom |

1958

| 27 November | Berlin Ultimatum: the Soviet Union terminates occupation and Four Power status of Berlin |

1959

| 11 May–20 June, 13 July–5 Aug. | Foreign Ministers' Conference of the Four Powers in Geneva, attended by delegations from FRG and GDR |

1960

| 16–17 May | Failure of Paris Summit Conference |

1961

| 3–4 June | Kennedy and Khruschev meet in Vienna |
| 13 August | Building of the Berlin Wall |

1962

| 22–28 Oct. | Cuban Crisis |

1963

| 17 December | First agreement on trans-border travel between the GDR and the West Berlin Senate |

1964

| 12 June | Agreement on mutual military support between Soviet Union and GDR |

1969

| 28 October | Chancellor Brandt's government statement on readiness to negotiate on equal terms with the GDR ('Two states — one nation') |

1970

19 March	Meeting between Brandt and Chairman of GDR Council of Ministers Stoph in Erfurt, East Germany
21 May	Brandt–Stoph meeting in Kassel, West Germany
12 August	Signing of German-Soviet Treaty in Moscow

7 December	Signing of German-Polish Treaty in Warsaw

1971

3 September	Signing of the (Four Power) Quadripartite Agreement on Berlin
17 December	Signing of Transit Agreement between FRG and GDR

1972

21 December	Signing of the Basic Treaty between the GDR and FRG in East Berlin

1973

18 September	Both FRG and GDR become members of the United Nations
11 December	Signing of Prague Treaty between FRG and Czechoslovakia

1975

30 July–1 Aug.	Concluding phase of Council for Security and Cooperation in Europe (CSCE) in Helsinki

1979

12 December	NATO Twin-track decision taken in Brussels

1981

11–13 Dec. (GDR)	Meeting between West German Chancellor Schmidt and East German Premier Honecker at the Werbellinsee (GDR)

1984

4 September	Honecker postpones his visit to the FRG scheduled for October

1985

19–21 Nov.	Reagan–Gorbachev summit meeting in Geneva

1986

19–22 Feb.	Visit to Bonn by the President of the East German parliament, Horst Sindermann
6 May	Signing of Cultural Agreement between Bonn Government and East German Government
11–12 Oct.	Reagan–Gorbachev summit meeting in Reykjavik

1987

7–11 Sept.	Honecker becomes the First East German leader to visit the FRG
9–11 Dec.	Reagan–Gorbachev summit meeting in Washington

Select Bibliography

Becker, Josef, and Andreas Hillgruber (eds.), *Die Deutsche Frage im 19. und 20. Jahrhundert*, Munich, 1983

Bender, Peter, *Das Ende des ideologischen Zeitalters. Die Europäisierung Europas*, Cologne, 1984

Benz, Wolfgang, et al., *Einheit der Nation. Diskussionen und Konzeptionen zur Deutschlandpolitik der grossen Parteien seit 1945*, Stuttgart, 1978

Blumenwitz, Dieter, and Boris Meissner (eds.), *Das Selbstbestimmungsrecht der Völker und die deutsche Frage*, Cologne, 1984

Boockmann, Hartmut, et al., *Mitten in Europa. Deutsche Geschichte*, Berlin, 1984

Brigouleix, Bernard, and Joseph Rovan (eds.), *Que devient l'Allemagne?*, Paris, 1986

Calleo, David, *The German Problem Reconsidered. Germany and the World Order, 1870 to the Present*, Cambridge, 1978

Craig, Gordon, *The Germans*, New York, 1982

Fritsch-Bournazel, Renata, et al., *Les Allemands au coeur de l'Europe*, Paris, 1983

Gasteyger, Curt, *Die beiden deutschen Staaten in der Weltpolitik*, Munich, 1976

Grosser, Alfred, *L'Allemagne en Occident. La République fédérale 40 ans après*, Paris, 1985

Hofer, Walther (ed.), *Europa und die Einheit Deutschlands. Eine Bilanz nach 100 Jahren*, Cologne, 1970

Jacobsen, Hans-Adolf, et al., *Drei Jahrzehnte Aussenpolitik der DDR. Bestimmungsfaktoren, Instrumente, Aktionsfelder*, Munich/Vienna, 1979

Jesse, Eckhard (ed.), *Bundesrepublik Deutschland und Deutsche Demokratische Republik. Die beiden deutschen Staaten im Vergleich*, Bonn, 1980

Kiersch, Gerhard, *Die jungen Deutschen. Die Erben von Goethe und Auschwitz*, Leverkusen, 1986

Le Gloannec, Anne-Marie, *1961. Un mur à Berlin*, Brussels, 1985

Löwenthal, Richard, and Hans-Peter Schwarz (eds.), *Die zweite Republik. 25 Jahre Bundesrepublik Deutschland — eine Bilanz*, Stuttgart, 1979

Noelle-Neumann, Elisabeth, *Eine demoskopische Deutschstunde. Texte, Thesen*, Zurich, 1983

Picht, Robert (ed.), *Deutschland – Frankreich – Europa. Bilanz einer schwierigen Partnerschaft*, Munich, 1978

Plessner, Helmut, *Die verspätete Nation. Ueber die politische Verführbarkeit bürgerlichen Geistes*, Frankfurt a.Main, 1974

Poidevin, Raymond, *L'Allemagne et le monde au XXème siècle*, Paris, 1983

Pross, Helge, *Was ist heute deutsch? Wertorientierungen in der Bundesrepublik*, Reinbek, 1982

Rovan, Joseph, *L'Allemagne du changement*, Paris, 1983

Schulz, Eberhard, *Die deutsche Nation in Europa. Internationale und historische Dimensionen*, Bonn, 1982

——, and Peter Danylow, *Bewegung in der deutschen Frage? Die ausländischen Besorgnisse über die Entwicklung in den beiden deutschen Staaten*, Bonn, 1985, 2nd ed.

Schwarz, Hans-Peter, *Vom Reich zur Bundesrepublik. Deutschland im Widerstreit der aussenpolitischen Konzeptionen in den Jahren der Besatzungsherrschaft 1945–1949*, Stuttgart, 1980, 2nd ed.

Schweigler, Gebhard, *Nationalbewusstsein in der BRD und in der DDR*, Düsseldorf, 1973

Schweitzer, Carl Christoph (ed.), *Die deutsche Nation. Aussagen von Bismarck bis Honecker*, Cologne, 1976

Spittmann-Rühle, Ilse, and Gisela Helwig (eds.), *Die beiden deutschen Staaten im Ost-West-Verhältnis*, Cologne, 1982

Szabo, Stephen F. (ed.), *The Successor Generation: International Perspectives of Postwar Europeans*, London, 1983

Weidenfeld, Werner (ed.), *Die Identität der Deutschen*, Munich, 1983

——(ed.), *Nachdenken über Deutschland. Materialien zur politischen Kultur der deutschen Frage*, Cologne, 1985

Weigelt, Klaus (ed.), *Heimat und Nation. Zur Geschichte und Identität der Deutschen*, Mainz, 1984

Weizsäcker, Richard von, *Die deutsche Geschichte geht weiter*, Berlin, 1983

Index